THE
SECRET LIVES
OF TEACHERS

THE
SECRET LIVES
OF TEACHERS

Anonymous

THE UNIVERSITY OF CHICAGO PRESS

Chicago and London

Anonymous is a high school history teacher in New York.

The University of Chicago Press, Chicago 60637
The University of Chicago Press, Ltd., London
© 2015 by The University of Chicago
All rights reserved. Published 2015.
Printed in the United States of America

24 23 22 21 20 19 18 17 16 15   1 2 3 4 5

ISBN-13: 978-0-226-31362-7 (cloth)
ISBN-13: 978-0-226-31376-4 (e-book)
DOI: 10.7208/chicago/9780226313764.001.0001

Library of Congress Cataloging-in-Publication Data
Dewey, Horace (Pseudonym), author.
The secret lives of teachers / Anonymous.
    pages ; cm
Includes bibliographical references.
ISBN 978-0-226-31362-7 (cloth : alk. paper) —
ISBN 978-0-226-31376-4 (ebook) 1. High school teach-
ers—New York (State)—New York. 2. Private schools—
New York (State)—New York. I. Title.
LB1777.3.N4D49 2016
373.110209747'1—dc23

2015020385

To the memory of

THEODORE R. SIZER (1932–2009)

Horace lives

The subordinate stature of classroom teachers is vividly symbolized by the roster of participants in these recurring academic brawls; the amplified voices have belonged to university presidents, freelance writers, eminent scholars, professors of education, leading citizens and even an admiral of the United States Navy. But who recalls hearing the opinions of a classroom teacher?

Dan Lortie, *Schoolteacher* (1975)

CONTENTS

Author's Note, xi

Introduction: Working Propositions, 3

SCHOOL'S OPEN
Commencing (*opening day*), 13

THE TEACHER WITHIN
Checking Your Self (*badges of identity*), 19
Compensations (*money, salary, and working conditions*), 25
Teaching Time (*seconds to decades*), 35
Subject Matters (*the role of academic disciplines*), 46
Progressive Faith (*the default philosophy of teachers*), 58

AMONG STUDENTS
Name Games (*the struggle to know one's students*), 73
Jealousy (*dealing with tears*), 84
Transit (*apprehending student lives in motion*), 92
Gradients (*assessments and their pitfalls*), 94
Romantics (*love in various forms*), 107
Questioning (*the role of classroom dialogue*), 111
Gingerly Revising (*confronting limits*), 120
Native Intelligence (*working with unprepared students*), 125
(Dangerous) Diversity (*touchy subjects and hurt feelings*), 130
Projection (*visiting another school*), 142
Enlarging the World (*the struggle to affirm the life of the mind*), 151

AMONG PARENTS

Parental Teaching (*the parent-teacher power struggle*), 163

Home Work (*managing family management*), 171

AMONG COLLEAGUES

Smart Board, Dumb Teacher (*technology and its discontents*), 185

Positions (*conflicts between teachers*), 190

AMONG ADMINISTRATORS

Complaints (*the faculty–administration divide*), 203

Brownie Points (*problem-solving / student discipline*), 220

SCHOOL'S CLOSE

Regraduating (*closing the circle*), 233

Afterword: A Note on Context, 237

Acknowledgments, 245

Notes, 247

AUTHOR'S NOTE

I greet you anonymously, dear reader. But as a practical matter, I need an identity for the pages that follow. I therefore declare myself Horace Dewey, history teacher at (fictive) East Hudson High School in New York City. As you will surely surmise, my pseudonym has symbolic significance. "Dewey" is an act of homage to John Dewey, the twentieth-century patron saint of progressive education (and a man whose influence remains vast, whether or not teachers work at progressive schools or even think of themselves as progressive). You might think that "Horace" is a nod toward Horace Mann, the nineteenth-century architect of the modern public school system, an allusion I won't disavow, as I am an admirer of his. But my first name is actually a tribute to the protagonist of Theodore R. Sizer's renowned Horace Trilogy, published between 1984 and 1996 and still widely discussed in educational circles to this day.

Though this is not a work of sensationalism or settling scores, it is one where I am more candid than is generally politic for a working teacher. More importantly, I have the privacy of students to protect. That is why names, situations, and identities in the following stories, set in the Obama era, have been changed or scrambled. I have also resorted to outright invention in some cases, though everything I describe here is rooted in more than a quarter-century's experience of classroom teaching, as well as some of the educational research cited in the afterword. My credibility lies in the truth of my storytelling.   "H.D."

THE
SECRET LIVES
OF TEACHERS

INTRODUCTION
Working Propositions

For many years, my colleague Bob Oros offered a history elective at my school called "The Working Class." The course covers an enormous range of territory, from the Spartacus Revolt in the Roman Republic to contemporary sweatshop labor. But more than anything else, Bob's class is an experience in what might be termed urban anthropology. His first assignment calls for students to go forth into their respective neighborhoods and observe people working. Upon identifying an occupation and a worker willing to talk, students are required to interview that person and take some pictures. They are then to produce a photo essay about the worker's occupation, with captioned pictures of the workers in action. Years ago, students used disposable cameras; nowadays they use their phones.

This assignment struck me as a good idea in the abstract. But the finished products I saw were stunning. I say this not because the quality of student work was so good (though there were many fine projects) but rather because the implicit message of the assignment was so palpable: there is simply no such thing as unskilled labor. The workers who came to life before my eyes in this assignment didn't necessarily love their jobs. But even seemingly simple occupations proved to have complications and nuances that aren't obvious when, say, you're ordering a burger and fries (be careful not to do X; always make sure you do Y, but not if there's a Z involved). I've never looked at work in quite the same way since. Nowadays I often try to strike up conversations with the workers I encounter on any given day and query them about the nature of their routines — unless it's obvious, even to me, that doing so is making me a pain in the ass.

Bob has another assignment in which students are asked to write a paper tracing the existence of a consumer product back to its source. One student chose a custom-made shawl that his mother and a few colleagues had chipped in to buy for a colleague recently diagnosed with cancer. He went to the boutique in midtown Manhattan where it had been commissioned, talking with the owner and manager of the store and following them into its back rooms, where immigrants from Taiwan and mainland China, laboring long hours in a high-end business, spoke with what he described as "a vague sense of escape in their voice." He heard a story from a manager of the seamstresses, a woman who had tried to start a business in China but could not succeed because of her gender (she described one customer who simply walked out upon learning that the store was hers). The student also heard about a worker whose health problems slowed her down but whose colleagues covered for her until she left the company to care for a grandchild. Toward the end of the piece, he turns his attention back to the final product. "A turquoise shawl lays across the table in the show room," he wrote. "There are bright colors that scream for attention all throughout the room and it looks like it belongs. Made of cashmere, it is exceptionally soft. It is warm, yet not overly hot. Finding the seams that keep it together is a job for Scooby Doo and the gang. The perfection was not easy to achieve, but it has been." Not bad for a high schooler. But I suppose I would think so: the student is my son.

I mention Bob's class, and my son's experience in it, by way of explaining how it is that I am now trying to explain my own job. It's not any more fascinating than anybody else's. But I now believe all jobs are of intrinsic interest, because they're always about a great many more things than whatever task is at hand. The trick—a piece of work in its own right—is figuring out a way to get at those things, whether they involve geopolitics, shifts in public attitudes, or the compromises that sometimes must be made in balancing conflicting imperatives.

Finding the right mode of discussion is a particularly vexing challenge in the case of teaching. Unlike some occupations, it engenders a good deal of curiosity. A lot of people have ideas about teaching, and a lot of those ideas involve how to get teachers to do their jobs better. Or how to find more good teachers. Or how to get around the need for them. There's nothing inherently wrong with any of this; many people engaged such enterprises have honorable motives. The problem is that relatively few of them have ever been teachers themselves (and almost by definition these few have not been teachers for any length of time—reformers are often too busy working on systems to actually perform the workaday tasks of teaching). And while it's possible for nonteachers to understand what teachers do all day, identifying and retaining good ones is more than a matter of monitoring the results of standardized tests.

It's a measure of how contentious some of the issues swirling around public education have become that some readers will see this as staking out a political position rather than simply stating the obvious. As a famous magazine article argued a few years back, it's about as hard to predict who will be a good teacher as it is to figure out who will be a good National Football League quarterback.[1]

I'm not seeking to create a mystique around teachers, any more than I would want others to create one around real estate agents, computer programmers, or hospital administrators. In all these cases, there *is* a certain mystery that defies easy analysis for the most successful ones: some people are just very, very good at these jobs, better than most of their peers.[2] Usually it's those peers who know better than anyone else who these people are. But each of these occupations involves a clearly identifiable set of skills, seasoning, and rituals that will be familiar to anyone in that craft. And, it's crucial to note, success in each of them will involve some degree of luck. It's the shared and plausibly attainable aspect of my profession that I'm interested in here, however.

But I'm not exactly a typical teacher. For the last fifteen years I have taught at an elite private school in New York City, where entrance to prekindergarten is more statistically challenging than entrance to any Ivy League college, and many of whose graduates in any given year will be admitted to those Ivy League colleges. (In fact, the school is part of a Greater New York consortium of independent schools informally known as the Ivy League.) This means that in a number of important respects my situation is atypical. My working conditions are highly favorable: whether measured by the quality of my students or the quality of the food in the cafeteria, I am a deeply fortunate man. The pay is good — by some reckonings, ridiculously good. Discipline is generally not a problem. Above all, I have a considerable degree of autonomy in what I teach and how I teach it. Parents are demanding, but they're interesting people who generally either are grateful for financial assistance — about a quarter of our students receive it — or want to believe that the approximately $900,000 it will cost to send child entering in 2015 from pre-K through twelfth grade is worth it.[3] My good fortune extends to areas that are not easily quantifiable or controllable: I have wonderful colleagues, and my bosses, who tend to turn over more quickly than my colleagues do, have been at least competent.

To be sure, we have our share of office politics, which I try to avoid—and one of my luxuries is that I've largely been able to do so.

All of this would seem to suggest that my experience is of limited relevance to the great majority of high school teachers or those interested in knowing more about them. (Though it should be said that schools like mine seem to attract no small amount of attention, to judge from the number of stories that crop up in publications like the *New York Times* on topics that range from their exclusivity to the scandals that periodically erupt into view.) Actually, I have little in the way of advice to dispense, not only because I'm aware of at least some of my limitations but also because I know that any pronouncements on my part are more likely to be ignored than rejected, let alone embraced. And yet there are two, perhaps paradoxical, reasons why the things I'd like to talk about in this book may be of value to teacher and nonteacher alike.

The first—and to my mind less important—reason is that my experience offers a real-life, nontheoretical example of what does and doesn't happen in a school where money is effectively no object. People who find themselves in underresourced schools may well wonder *which* resource is the most valuable: is it small class size? academic support from learning specialists? the ability to remove problem students? freedom from excessive administrative supervision? My job is effectively a case study because I have about as much of such finite resources as anybody ever gets. You can ask yourself: Does what happens at my school happen at yours? *Should* what happens at my school happen at yours? Why or why not?

I am by no means implying that my colleagues and I always get things right. We don't, and I make some effort to document my own mistakes in particular. Sometimes they're specific errors in execution; other times they reflect my limitations as a man of my time and place; in still others they're a function of institutional choices and tradeoffs in a school culture that's larger than any one of us. One of the biggest tensions at my school is a collective desire to nurture the whole child while serving simultaneously as a preparatory academy that maintains its track record in placing graduates in selective colleges and universities—which is the main, though not only, reason parents are willing to make the financial and other sacrifices necessary to send a child to a private school like mine. Cooperation and competition, sanctioned and not, jostle every day. We strive for equality—the school is proud of the depth and breadth of its diversity, albeit of a highly manicured kind—but the very essence of the institution is exclusion, a reality we all know and yet try to avoid, even deny.

This tension is further intensified by the fact that my school bills itself as a progressive institution. As I explain in one of my chapters, the word *progressive* means a great many things to a great many people, some of them contradictory (and many of them embraced by people who do not think of themselves as progressive—who indeed are avowed critics of progressive education). Progressives are child-centered with an emphasis on experiential learning; they're also policy wonks that like to orchestrate environments and shape consciousness. Such differences, and the gradations between them, often conflict within the same school—and within the same person.

Which brings me to the second, and to my mind more decisive, theme of this book. Fallibility, conflict, and finite resources are not simply realities at my school; they're universal conditions at all schools. So are wisdom, cooperation, and generosity, which can be found at even the most literally or figuratively impoverished ones. One of the paradoxes of teaching is that, as University of Chicago professor Philip W. Jackson put it in his now-classic *Life in Classrooms*, "school is school, no matter where it happens."[4] Whatever the wrinkles, variations, or exceptions, school almost always means age-graded collections of children segmented into rooms for discrete periods, whether they want to be there or not — something that has been true since the time of Horace Mann almost two centuries ago. And school means teachers who, however much they, their superiors, or reformers may wish otherwise, play an indispensable role in supervising what happens on their watch (and whose influence resonates afterward — sometimes long afterward).[5] There may come a time when at least some of this work may be done virtually. And we're now in a time when there is a growing effort to centralize curriculum management and require teachers to collaborate more closely. But such developments have not yet fundamentally changed the underlying dynamics of schooling, any more than the advent of movies ended the role of books (or campfires) in storytelling.

It is these shared, yet personal, aspects of the teaching life that I'm trying to capture in these pages. Writing two decades after *Life in Classrooms* was published, Jackson noted that "the effect of being awakened to the complexities of schooling, at least as I have experienced it, is to see *both* the praiseworthy and the blameworthy, not as mutually exclusive categories of events demanding immediate action or commendation but as we find them elsewhere in life — curiously interdependent and frustratingly intertwined."[6] Jackson was trying to understand these complexities in the spirit of an ethnographer looking from the outside in. I'm writing from the inside out, describing a consciousness as much as a set of circumstances.

What kind of consciousness and circumstances? The ones

that tend not to find their way into most books about teachers. Things like teacher attitudes toward money. And clothing. Or the kinds of things that a teacher is thinking—but not saying—when talking with a student, a colleague, or a parent. A teacher's sense of time. Envy and longing, admiration and affection. Fear and hope. And uncertainty about such things, which are often operating simultaneously, and sometimes subliminally.

The perspective from which I write is my own, describing that which I have heard, seen, and sensed. I'm certainly not representative in my take on such matters; just as certainly, I'm not unique. What I'm striving for is not a matter of avenging slights or sensationalizing the mundane. Nor is it a set of policy prescriptions. Instead I seek to articulate a set of issues and provisional answers that readers can discuss and make sense of in their own way.

Shall we proceed?

SCHOOL'S OPEN

COMMENCING

Morning, first day of school, our opening assembly convenes outside. The student body, seated on the grass, chatters on the sun-dappled quad; my colleagues dot the rim. Summer heat and humidity linger; the collar on my new white oxford shirt is already damp.

Down at the podium, a series of speakers go through their paces. Our principal, the redoubtable Hannah Osborne, welcomes the student body back and gives a special nod to the seniors, who whoop it up: their Moment has come. The senior class presidents — white male, black female, typical of winning political combinations in the past few years — make announcements, all of which are met with disproportionate enthusiasm, some of it sarcastic. Literally and figuratively, we've all been here before, but nobody seems to mind.

My gaze shifts to the broader sweep of the student body. I feel a combination of envy and pity — recapturing that sense of promise would be nice, but boy am I glad most aspects of my own adolescence are behind me. I look into the faces of these students and imagine them as middle aged. Some, I think, will weather well; in others I see sagging jaws and wan expressions.

In the center of the crowd, embedded in the senior grass, I see my former student Jared Black. He eked out a B– in my class last spring; my colleague in the science department, Carl Kaminisky, told me Jared had been in his office in tears the day after his failure to hand in a lab report triggered an academic probation that threatened to keep him off the lacrosse field during conference finals. I don't know what became of that, but Jared could not look more comfortable than he does right now with his backwards baseball cap, sunglasses, and arm around Katie Fontaine. This disappoints me: I always thought of Katie as a level-headed girl.

Off to the right is Marcus Cassidy, now a junior, isolated in the crowd, plucking grass and probably wishing he were anywhere else. High school can't end fast enough for Marcus. After he was caught cheating on a Spanish exam in June, Hannah decided against disciplinary action — his overbearing single father and evident self-loathing made anything beyond an F on the test seem like piling on. Actually, I've got some hope for Marcus. He's fairly intelligent; Dad's unrealistic expectations notwithstanding (no doubt a factor in the cheating), he'll probably get into a decent college. His skin will improve, and I can imagine him putting a few pounds on his slender frame. I picture an appealingly incredulous fiancée a decade from now trying to imagine him as the ungainly kid he currently is, her momentary flash of dismay giving way to instinctive affection. She'll laugh at the thought of him as a dweeb, and maybe he will, too.

Behind Marcus, further still to the right are Jill Hansen and Ella Vaccaro. They've been inseparable ever since middle school. Sometimes as I head home I see them on the quad, quietly conversing as they sit on the stone wall that marks the quad's northern boundary. Other times they'll be reading silently, their presence an evident comfort to each other even as they seem immersed in their books. There will be all kinds of forces in the coming months and years to pull them apart, but something tells me their bond is going to last across space and time.

And Jenny Tindall — my God, she's beautiful. Looking at her is like staring into the sun. There are probably dozens of boys that go tongue-tied just at the thought of her. Reminds me a bit of Jessie Hecht. I admired Jessie's poise from afar until she ended up in my Civil War elective, at which point I learned she was an emotional wreck whose depression crippled her to the point where she had to drop out of school for a semester (she ended up with a C in my class, a gift). I don't think Jenny has those problems. I wonder how long her beauty will last. Maybe another couple decades. In the scheme of a lifetime that may not be much, but to her at least it would have to seem like a long time, especially right now. I'd like to think that the memory of her pulchritude will endow her with a confidence and security that will sustain her beyond her youth.

At the far end of the crowd I see Marybeth Ianuzzi for the first time in months. She's just finished her second round of chemo — the first was last spring, followed by another this summer. Always elegant, she's wrapped a scarf around her head that almost seems like more of a fashion choice than a concession to the ravages of her disease. I hope that Shakespeare course of hers will be a blessed distraction from her encroaching mortality. I need to go over and give her a proper hello later. Will she even be here come graduation?

All right, you guys, have a good year, Hannah is saying. (How much longer will "you guys" be considered an appropriate salutation, I wonder.) The buoyant chatter returns as the gathering disperses. I've got about forty minutes before my first class. One last bout of hurry up and wait. The beginning always takes forever to arrive.

THE TEACHER WITHIN

CHECKING YOUR SELF

When I turn around to check the time, I see it's 6:43 a.m. I've been rooted here in my underwear in front of my closet for a solid six minutes — far too long. This was supposed to be easy. It's Friday, which means I get to wear my favorite faded blue jeans and my solid navy cotton shirt. The question has been which tie should go with them. Even though it's early in the semester, I've already gone through some of my favorites — the one with Beatles album covers, the one with the Gettysburg Address, the Van Gogh *Starry Night*. What's left? There's Shrek, but that goes better with my black or khaki jeans. Ditto for the Chinese food. I love that Paul Klee my wife bought for me at the Metropolitan Museum of Art last summer, but that would be breaking a self-imposed rule, since I've worn it already this semester. There's Superman, which gets lots of positive comments, but I always feel a little immodest wearing it, as if I'm implying *I'm* Superman. I could go for a more low-key approach — red polka dots on a field of royal blue, or the metallic paisley of red, blue, and silver. But today is a full day, and since I'm teaching most of my classes, I'd like to don something from what I consider my A list.

Ah-ha — I remember I'm giving a unit test in my humanities course today. I finger my way through one of the racks on the closet wall looking for the tie with the pair of dice. I'll imply that taking a test is a game of chance. Then I encounter something even better: Edvard Munch's *The Scream* — the guy on the bridge with his hands over his ears in a silent wail. Now *that* seems apropos for a test. Let's see if anyone gets the joke.

Schools have varying rules about couture for faculty as well as students, but one way or another everybody wears a uniform. When left to their own devices, teachers usually opt for the informal, men (as usual) having more leeway, principally in the form of less censure for slovenliness. Sometimes clothes make an ideological statement, most commonly when teachers affirm their class politics by dressing down. Other times fashion reflects complacency, if not sloth: my job is secure and there's no one I need to impress. (It irks me to see my colleague Mark Van Ness in the Foreign Languages Department, who often wears shorts on the job.) Very often couture is a matter of pragmatism; in a job where you spend a lot of time on your feet, for example, sensible shoes prevail. Of course these and other motives mingle, as do manifold exceptions. A few of my colleagues dress beautifully, and I will occasionally compliment them, at other times silently admiring the power of their packaging. But however stylish they may be, teachers rarely dress like doctors, lawyers, or other professionals, and while few are foolish enough to chase adolescent style, the choices of students do exert a gravitational pull, which is precisely why some schools impose rules on both (and why both will try to stretch them).

I'm a fairly typical specimen in this regard. In the first years of my job as a high school teacher, I wore khakis, a dress shirt, a tie, and work shoes. More recently I've lapsed back toward jeans and cords, retaining the shoes and (especially) the ties, which have become more colorful as my cotton shirts have turned toward earth tones. The ties have become my signature — most in my large and growing collection are gifts, and I only half-jokingly call them antisoporific devices. They're like a shaft of personality I allow to escape my otherwise unprepossessing casing.

The act of getting dressed in the morning—in particular, the act of threading my belt and filling my pockets—is one of the most satisfying rituals of my day. There's a fixed sequence: keys on the left, phone on the right, comb back left, and wallet back right. Peppermint Altoid smalls in the change pocket. I glide a lacquered pen (another indulgence) into my shirt pocket. My watch clips onto a belt loop, a legacy of carpal tunnel syndrome. On the belt itself goes my photo ID, a requirement that arose in the wake of school shootings around the country and a reminder of the price we pay in prioritizing the freedom of gun owners over that of children. But I'd be lying if I didn't confess that I regard that plastic card as a satisfying piece of armor for battle. Sometimes as I dress I imagine the lipstick rolling, the shirts buttoning, and the boots zipping as my fellow travelers converge on the building we share.

Among contemporary multicultural educators and consultants, there's a discourse about the problem of students (and, in some cases, faculty) having to "check your identity at the door." It addresses the fact that there's often a minority—racial, sexual, socioeconomic, religious, disabled—that feels obliged to conform to the dominant culture of a school, and to downplay, even deny, the realities of their own lives. This conflict continues when they return home, as they "code-switch" between their communities of origin and the ones they're being socialized to join. In private schools in particular, administrators and parents strive to close this gap through tools like creating affinity groups and quietly awarding subsidies for field trips.

At the risk of some presumption, I'll say that I have at least some idea about what these people are trying to do, because as a first-generation college student with growing awareness that many of my peers lived decidedly different lives than I did, I experienced such tensions firsthand. I don't insist those tensions be passively accepted by students or those trying to help them. That said, I believe there are times and ways when there is nothing more liberating than checking your self at the door. When I enter a building literally bearing my identity as a teacher, the school logo trumps the idiosyncrasies of my face and all the other particularities of my life—among them that tie, an affectation likely to be ignored by others and forgotten by me. Once I'm at work, I have a set of privileges and responsibilities that offer the promise of relief from self-consciousness. That promise isn't always realized, of course, because outside forces (like a phone call from home) disrupt it. Still, the mere prospect of losing oneself in one's work is among the most precious assets of the gainfully employed.

But it's not only the employed who experience it. The particularities of identity formation notwithstanding, students also savor checking their identities at the door and becoming members of the mass, whether it's that of a school, a class, or a team. Is there any talisman of collective identity more savored than the team jersey or varsity jacket?

One of the most valuable aspects of checking your identity at the door is the way your memory of having done so remains long after the day is over. In some respects this is humbling—the person in that bathrobe you see in the mirror is usually a good deal less impressive than the one you see after you get dressed. A similar laxity extends to behavior. More than once I've winced, after yelling at my kids or doing something else I regretted, when I imagined my students witnessing what I've just said or done. Ironically, playing a role can keep you honest.

It also has its guilty pleasures. When I was the father of young children and subject to the demands of *that* role, the promise of a working day at school felt like freedom. Days or weeks off—and the absence of daycare that usually accompanied them—loomed large. These days, I savor a snow day or three-day weekend as much as any of my colleagues do, even if my pastimes are of the most quotidian kind. But pending burdens, like long-term illness or aging parents, are always around to remind me that a job can feel like a vacation.

Each of us is a repertory company: we're not really functional, much less happy, unless we're playing a variety of parts. And changing costumes. Most of the time we're handed our scripts. The rest is a matter of interpretation—and impersonation.

🐾🐾🐾

"Ooooh, *The Scream*—I *love* it," my colleague Denise Richardson, who teaches English, tells me while we wait on line for a cup of coffee before the first class of the day. "Feeling a little suicidal today, Horace?"

"Nope. Test this afternoon."

"How lovely. I'm sure your students will appreciate your solicitude."

But they don't seem to notice. When I enter the room, most of the girls seem freaked out, poring over study guides and querying each other on the main provisions of the Mayflower Compact. I'm asked a few stray questions, which I answer as I arrange desks into rows, something I suspect reassures some of the students even as it may frustrate others. The exam goes off without a hitch; I'm asked some leading questions by students seeking to wring a few points out of me ("What does 'predestination' mean?"; "When you say 'the Virginia Company' do you mean a business or just a group of people?"), which I try to deflect as best I can. I always end up saying more than I want to.

The last person to finish is Kim Anders, who's double- (or triple- or quadruple-) checking her work even as students from the next class are gathering just beyond the closed door, peering in as a hint that it's time for her to clear out so they can get in.

"I saw that painting recently at the Museum of Modern Art," she says, gesturing at my tie as she approaches me at the front of the room. "I went with my dad. What's his name — Edward Mensch?"

"Munch."

"*The Scream*, right?"

"Right."

"Is that supposed to be a joke?"

"Kinda."

Kim nods, mirthlessly. Then she walks over to the door, puts her hands to her ears, and issues a brief, punctuated scream: "HAAAA!" The kids on the other side of the door flinch. After the initial terror, a few laugh; others look at her angrily.

Kim turns back me as she opens the door to exit. "Thanks, Mr. Dewey."

"For what? You like taking tests?"

Kim squints, considering the question. "Ummm, I dunno. The tie, I guess. I like it."

"I should be thanking you," I say with a smile. But Kim is already washed away amid the incoming tide.

COMPENSATIONS

I stare at the calculator: $281.92. That's what I have to work with in terms of a car payment. My wife, a soccer mom who totes three kids (a fourth is in college) and a couple of dogs all over metropolitan New York — about two thousand miles a month — drives too much to lease one. We'll have to buy — hopefully new, maybe used. But $281.92 a month for five years will get us only about halfway there. She and I have been doing extra work — summer classes, SAT II prep, and so on — to make up the difference (and pay for a looming set of braces on our youngest).

I find all this exhausting, even depressing, to contemplate. I shouldn't. My salary has gone up substantially over the course of the last decade, thanks to a series of good contracts and my recent appointment as department chair. I now make well more than double the $48,000 I did when I started at the school in 2001, breaking through to the sixth figure in my salary shortly after my promotion. I am — by most measures of most jobs — well paid. Alas, I deploy my assets as soon as they appear.

I have three major expenses. The first is tuition for two of my children; even with a substantial staff discount, it comes to about $32,400 of my after-tax earnings. The rest of my paycheck goes to our mortgage payment ($27,600 annually) and property taxes ($17,000), which I gladly pay since I have a learning-disabled child in a good public school system. That's most of my take-home pay, leaving the salary of my wife, a tenured professor at a nearby liberal arts college who makes less than I do, to cover most of the rest of our expenses, with the significant exception of my eldest child's college tuition, covered thanks to the generosity and foresight of my in-laws. We spend too much on takeout and too little on things like home maintenance (our house steadily becomes shabbier—cracks in the driveway, fingerprints on the walls, a running battle against mildew in our bathrooms). And we don't give enough to charity. A new minivan has already been deferred a couple times, and waiting much longer would be asking for a harrowing breakdown on the highway with kids and or dogs in the old one.

I tell you these fairly quotidian details about my financial situation in part because it's the kind of thing my peers just don't talk about. (Contemporary Americans seem more candid about their orgasms than about their finances.) But I believe my circumstances—and, more important, my attitudes—are typical of educators of my generation and point in the life cycle. The proportion of my income that goes to my children's schooling, for example, is an amount many people would consider absurd. But I reckon we all have our indulgences, and mine is typical of my profession. Like a great many Americans, I experience myself as middle class, whether or not the facts warrant such a designation. I do think, with the support of some expert opinion I find in the business section of the *New York Times* and other publications that I regularly graze, that supporting such a lifestyle is more expensive than it used to be. I live better than my parents, a housewife and a New York City firefighter, did when I was growing up (indeed, as a late baby boomer I'm a vanishing specimen of the American Dream). But my upward mobility has been tempered by the rate of inflation for things like housing and education. And having four kids? Financially speaking, that's just stupid.

Whatever the pay scale, few jobs seem more quintessentially middle class than teaching. No one ever gets rich as a teacher. Still, while it's relatively low on the professional ladder, teaching is a bona fide career in a society where the middle is being whittled out of existence. Teachers are still generally on the right side of a jagged economic divide in that we receive salaries (not hourly wages), health care benefits, and paid vacation—a particularly prized perk of unusual duration. Teaching has been an actual profession for a little over a century now, a development spurred by a series of convergent phenomena: a Progressive movement that spurred professionalization in many occupations; the emergence of schools of education offering graduate degrees; and an influx of men taking what has often been considered "women's work."

As with so many other occupations in the twenty-first century, the economic foundations of teaching have been eroding, however, particularly in the growing number of communities quietly buckling under economic stress, as well as those insisting on quantitative measures of student performance as a basis of future employment. There have, moreover, always been tiers that fall short of steady, secure employment—teaching assistant jobs, substitute teaching, sabbatical or maternity leave appointments, and the like. Some of these occasionally lead to a full-time slot, but it's in the very nature of such positions that nothing is guaranteed. We can't escape—do we really want to escape?—hierarchical tiers in even the most level of socioeconomic landscapes.

Teaching has never had the prestige associated with law or medicine (though that of both has deteriorated in recent years), or the excitement associated with journalism (less professionally structured and not especially remunerative for most of its history, but alluring for its access to power and/or the spotlight). Nor does primary or secondary school teaching enjoy the stature associated with college or university

instruction, which has generally placed much more emphasis on producing original scholarship than on fostering the
art of pedagogy. In terms of social cachet, primary and secondary education has a relationship with the professoriate
that can be compared with that of nursing and medicine: as
nurses are to doctors, teachers are to professors. The former
are generalists who take care of what are perceived as the less
complicated cases, often knowing and doing more than they
get credit for, while the latter enjoy greater stature rooted
in longer years of study and specialization. (Again there are
gender echoes here, as teaching and nursing have long been
regarded as feminine "helping" professions).[1]

I speak as a failed academic. I went to graduate school in
the late 1980s and early 1990s, earning a PhD in American
studies. I held on for almost a decade in adjunct positions —
including a couple of very attractive ones, but all of them
dead ends. I might have held on longer had not the arrival
of children (among them an unexpected set of twins and an
even more medically surprising daughter) rendered the long-
distance commute I'd been doing untenable. It was time to
grow up and think seriously about making money. Lacking
the credentials to teach in public school, I was lucky to land
my current post; from the start I believed that it would likely
be the first and last real job I'd ever be offered. White, male,
old, and overpriced in a market that prizes youth and diversity, I'm probably unemployable anywhere else.

One other aspect of my good fortune is that I belong to a
union, something that's quite rare at a private school. From
time to time I'll hear people say that the teaching profession lost some of its luster with the rise of powerful unions
in the mid-twentieth century: educators traded away their
reputation as esteemed community leaders in favor of that of

employees collectively bargaining for higher pay and better benefits. There may be some truth to that (along with some overlooked realities about teachers being fired for their beliefs at the behest of petty principals, or simply to make room for someone's brother-in-law). But as far as I can tell, American teachers have never enjoyed the relative social esteem of those in other countries, particularly in Asia. This may have something to do with the sheer size and heterogeneity of the teaching labor force in a country with a student body as large and varied as this one: teachers are dime a dozen. It's a little staggering to consider that there are almost seventeen hundred public schools in New York City alone, with eighty-nine thousand educators serving over a million students.[2] If teaching were a rank in the military, it would be that of a private in the infantry (with students as the civilians).

Here's the thing: the United States has always funded its education system in a distinctive way, relying on communities to tax themselves, rather than treating education as primarily a matter of *national* policy, finance, and administration. This has resulted in a tremendous range in educational quality and a diverse array of private schools (sectarian, preparatory academies, et al.) along with an even more diverse array of public ones. It's also resulted in a tremendous range in pay scales — a starting teacher in Alabama or Mississippi makes a fraction of one in Connecticut or Massachusetts, and there are significant disparities within the latter states (consider the difference between impoverished Bridgeport and nearby Greenwich, whose schools are every bit as well appointed as the most pricey private academy). In the most affluent communities, like the one in which I work, teachers enjoy a status approaching that of some of their Finnish or Korean peers; in the most underresourced ones they are forced to endure any number of petty humiliations, financial and otherwise, which are likely to be visited even more aggressively upon students, especially in socioeconomically mixed communities where taxpayers resist what they perceive as subsidizing other people's children.[3]

But salaries are only one variable in measuring the value of teaching as a way to make a living. While my peers and I necessarily care about money — and sometimes we care very deeply, maybe more than we should — the principal appeal of the job is not really pecuniary. It is, rather, more about the general occupational *conditions* of the craft. What makes teaching a little different from most office work, for example, is that teachers tend to operate without much in the way of direct (or, at any rate, continuous) supervision. Though this can be exaggerated — there are often people of one kind or another passing through the classroom; collaboration with other faculty is often sought and attained; students and parents provide feedback to administrators, and all of these intervene in the educational process in one form or another — there is a powerful myth of the teacher as the ruler of a small domain, one that may be receding in public schools but that remains alive in private ones. This sense of control over the terms of one's work is among the most cherished features of the profession. Indeed, anything that is perceived as limiting or compromising it is often cited as a reason for leaving or retiring. Many teachers feel a sense of pride and ownership in their classrooms, which they decorate and organize to reflect their values no less than their pedagogy. So it is that you'll find Bruce Springsteen and Abraham Lincoln posters in my classroom, along with ticket stubs, newspaper clippings, and magnetic dolls of Harriet Tubman and F. Scott Fitzgerald (gifts of students).

Territorial encroachments, literal and figurative, are nevertheless virtually continuous. In recent years these have become more systematic via curriculum mapping and other forms of bureaucratic control. A series of mandates—departmental, administrative, state, and federal, notably the national Common Core standards—shape and limit teacher autonomy. The school schedule is another source of friction, ranging from instruction that must be shoehorned into a tight wedge of the school day to incidental disruptions like a homecoming pep rally or a string of snow days.

Then there are the power struggles that take place at the ground level: students who actively or passively resist working; those who overtly or surreptitiously distract others in the room; understandable or misplaced questions that impede the completion of the task at hand. So it is that the best-laid plans can go awry—assuming, of course, that there *are* plans, best-laid or otherwise, from which a teacher is working. Not having time to plan is among the perennial teacher complaints.

For some of us, such impediments can feel like sand in mental gears that gradually wear us down. But if a sense of autonomy gets lost—or was never really experienced in the first place—there has long been another source of solace in the profession: its relative insulation from the pressures of the marketplace. As occupations go, teaching is secure. It isn't easy to get a job, and there can be great anxiety in those years before tenure is attained. Once a teacher gets tenure, however, it's rare to be fired or be laid off, much as many parents, administrators, and school reformers may wish otherwise. (Again, in the age of No Child Left Behind this sense of security has eroded, though it's still substantial in many places.) A lot of this is a matter of the stakes seeming so high: it's easier to put up with mediocrity that's diffuse (and temporary — for the unhappy student, there's always next year) than to destroy someone's livelihood, particularly given the likelihood of downward mobility. Even when union rules aren't a factor, it can be hard to take that step, however justified, even necessary, it may be. I know this is very aggravating to people like my brother-in-law, a successful businessman who has trouble accepting my relative lack of accountability. In the end, though, I'm not sure we teachers are as complacent as we can sometimes seem. I've spent plenty of time awake in bed imagining nightmare scenarios wherein I am fired.

Teachers are generally a risk-averse bunch. We're liberal in our politics but conservative in our temperaments, preferring routine activities and safe returns than seeking a big, risky payoff. Whether or not we're actively hostile to capitalism, our paychecks tend to come from the public sector, and we tend to view market considerations with skepticism if not instinctive opposition. (My private school colleagues tend to loathe and resent the fact that their paychecks come from rich people.) This makes teachers out of touch in some respects. But we also help generate products in the form of people who will constitute a marketplace essential to the survival of the overall economy. That's literally priceless.

In any case, the perks of teaching are not solely a matter of the workplace. Though outsiders often fail to consider how much work must be done beyond the boundaries of the school day, the hours are incontestably attractive. Even if late afternoons, weekends, and summers are not "free" or "off," they nevertheless afford a degree of control over one's time that amounts to one more dimension of the autonomy teachers crave.

So it is that day becomes week becomes month becomes year becomes decade. The cyclical rhythms of school life can be one more appealing feature of the profession. But they can also seem like a trap, creating a countdown toward retirement in which time blurs and the kids keep getting more exhausting and you keep having less energy. At the same time, the steadiness of the work can breed complacency or listlessness as routines become oppressive and developing new ones seems even more tiresome. The key to sustaining oneself involves maintaining a sense of curiosity, not just about ideas but also about people. But that's not as simple as it sounds, because such matters may not be entirely a matter of choice: you can't always will yourself to be interested.

Insofar as one does have some control over the matter, sustaining vitality takes one of two forms. The first—which I suspect happens more with veteran teachers on the younger side of the ledger—involves cultivating a sense of professional ambition by trying new things, like developing a new class, attending conferences, or extending one's professional network closer to home. In a way, this is a matter of hedging one's bets, of having an investment in one's work that's not directly a matter of a school or a set of students. Such a hedge can insulate one from the day-to-day aggravations of the job even as it provides the plausible hope of paying off in some way down the road. Sometimes teachers develop passions that are outside—or at least initially *seem* outside—the job, which is a big part of their appeal: gardening, yoga, genealogy. Even here there may be possibilities of nurturing one's work, whether through content that can be adapted to the classroom in some way or a pedagogic approach that can be imported into one's teaching style.

The other source of sustenance—this one perhaps the domain of the aging geezers—comes from the opposite direction. This involves an appreciation of what one has rather than that which one will not attain, coupled with a newfound desire to achieve a sense of purpose by helping others. In this as in so much else, teaching is a profession of hope.

※§※

My gaze shifts back to the $281.92 on my calculator. That's $3,383.04 a year; over the course of a five-year loan it adds up to $16,902.20. Some portion of that would be interest. How much would depend on the rate. I'm getting close to the edge of my numeric competency in any case. I figure I'll need about $15,000 as a down payment. Damn. For thirty grand I could probably get a pretty nice sports car. Not this time.

A cousin of mine once cracked: "When a pretty girl smiles at you as you pull up at a light in a minivan, it's all you, man." I'm not in the market for pretty girls anymore. I'm just trying to get the job done — or, I should say, to do one job well enough and long enough to get another one, that of family man, done. Then, surely, I'll be on easy street, right?

TEACHING TIME

❦

Kendra Parks is standing to my left as I approach the buffet table at my school's annual holiday party. A dusky light filters through the window of the teacher's lounge; the chatter of my colleagues competes with the garlanded boom box projecting Bruce Springsteen's caterwauling version of "Santa Claus Is Coming to Town." So I have to raise my voice a little when I ask, "How's it going, Kendra?"

"Oh — hi, Horace!" she says, with real warmth in her voice, for which I'm grateful. I don't know Kendra well. She's a new hire in the math department, and the buzz about her that I hear from students is good. She looks to be on the cusp of thirty, which may well make her the youngest teacher at a school where a master's degree and a few years of teaching experience are usually prerequisites. I'm still sufficiently beholden to my segregated suburban childhood to find her dreadlocks — well, just what *is* it that I feel about them? Not intimidated, as I would have been thirty years ago. Not irritated, the way I might have felt twenty years ago, when I wrongly bristled at such identity assertion. Still, Kendra's riotous hair and dark skin feel like a foreign country, one where I felt a need to be slightly more careful in my observance of social custom than I otherwise would be. Off to my left I see the ninth-grade dean, Felicity Felson, a woman who, I learned last week, is, like me, fifty-one and with whom I feel, probably presumptuously, a generational affinity that bridges our difference in race and gender.

"So how are you holding up in your first semester?" I ask Kendra.

She exhales deeply and then flashes me a smile. "I'm fabulous. Fabulously exhausted."

"Well, you look pretty spry to me."

"Don't look too close!" she says with a laugh. "I've aged ten years in the last three months."

"Well, you're still a spring chicken in my book."

"Maybe," she says, biting into a stalk of celery. "You know how it is. The school year starts and then you blink and it's November. And then it's March. But it's all going by you in a blur while you're trying to grade tests, plan lessons, and figure out what you want to teach next year."

"It's hard the first time around." I realize I'm not exactly offering scintillating conversation, but given the noise level it would be foolish to move beyond small talk, even if I had any idea where to go with it.

"It *is* hard," she says, swallowing some bottled water. "I mean, I have some sense of the rhythm from my last school. And I actually kind of like it. Especially when we reach this moment—the day before the holiday vacation is my favorite day of the school year. Just knowing that I can go home and sleep for a week. It's delicious."

I'm trying to imagine Kendra's home when I feel a hand on my back. "There he is. Right in the front of the gravy train."

It's Harry Dugan, an old-timer in the English department. Harry is seventy-two and has been teaching here for over forty years. "How are you, Harry?"

"Better now," he says, winking at Kendra. "Friday afternoon. Doesn't get any better."

"Going away over the break?"

"Hilton Head," he says. "Janice and I are going to see our new granddaughter. Hoping to get in a little golf. Gotta prep for my retirement," he says, making a swinging motion.

Harry's been talking about retiring for years. I wonder

if he's finally getting serious about it. My colleague Denise Richardson says he's waiting for a buyout offer. I find myself wishing it would happen. I like Harry, but he's been here too long. I hear the kids joking about his tendency to regale the class with family anecdotes and make only minimal comments on their essays.

"Where do you play around here?" Kendra asks. Is she a golfer? *Do* black women golf?

"Oh, you know, over at Van Cortlandt Park, though sometimes I head over to Pelham for a round at Split Rock," he says. "You play?"

"Naaah," she says dismissively. "Back in college I was on a rec team."

"Oh yeah?" Harry is genuinely interested. "Where was that? What's your handicap?"

"Tufts. Wasn't any good. I was also a field hockey player. Goalie. NESCAC champs."

Harry nods approvingly. "When did you graduate?"

"Nine years ago. I just got the notice about my tenth reunion."

"Ah, school days," Harry says musingly. "Best years of my life."

"Haven't pretty much *all* your years been school years, Harry?" I ask.

"Exactly. Secret of life. Now if you kids will excuse me, I'm going to see if I can sneak into a bar with my fake ID."

※⁹²※

More than most professions, the work of teaching has a circular rhythm. The grooves run deep: every American over five years old has experienced the cycle of the school year repeatedly, and every parent reexperiences it in their offspring's childhood. Even people long finished with schooling in any form are often nostalgic about the beginnings of the school year each fall and the prospect of release that looms with the arrival of summer. Back-to-school sales, holiday vacations, and traffic patterns shape the annual calendar for all of us.

In fact, the cycles of the school year are a set of concentric circles whose smallest unit measure are periods — often demarcated by buzzers — that mark the school day. These generally run about forty-five minutes, though in schools with block schedules they can go twice that (as science labs do). In theory, at least, no two class sessions are alike; even when the lesson plan of the day involves review or reinforcement, the techniques and pacing are likely to vary. But their structure, whether that of a teacher addressing students, students working on their own, or students holding discussions among themselves, is likely to be experienced as ritualized. Neither teacher nor students are in class every minute of the school day — prep periods for teachers, study halls for students, and breaks for lunch and passing time are standard, even if ambitious students choose to stuff their days to the gills. But the size and shape of the breaks are determined by class schedule: free time is defined by class time.

A series of periods constitute a day, and a series of days constitute a week. Not all weeks proceed in a straight five-day fashion; some schools operate on a six-or-more-day schedule where the sequence of periods in a day alternates (for example, classes that meet Monday-Wednesday-Friday one week will meet Tuesday-Thursday the next). There will also be fixed elements in the weekly calendar — like Thursday-morning assemblies — that both provide a wrinkle in an otherwise monotonous weekly calendar and are routine at the same time.

In most American schools, classes almost are bounded by Monday mornings and Friday afternoons. Any number of other extracurricular activities, from athletic events to car washes, may be packed around the school day and spill into the weekend. But the academic core of the week is fixed, punctuated by a staccato rhythm of holidays, from single days to weeklong breaks in late December, midwinter, and spring. Some schools observe holidays such as Veterans Day on their original commemorative date (November 11) regardless where they fall in the week. But most have embraced the leisured logic of the three-day weekend, from Columbus Day to Memorial Day. These holidays have been almost entirely drained of any historical content; it's a little sad for commemorations of people like Martin Luther King Jr. to be reduced to an excuse for an extra day of skiing or a sale at the mall.

Sometimes the school year is experienced as a tunnel you enter in September and emerge from in June. For all the predictability that marks the calendar, it is in fact quite difficult for students or teachers to keep the flow of work in equilibrium: there are simply too many moving parts. Some weeks are easy — the tasks at hand are known and manageable. Other weeks are hard, with multiple deadlines arriving simultaneously. Some of these are curricular, like a pile of papers that need to be graded, their timing determined by the pace of the students and the length of the unit. Others are institutionally driven, like the demand for data for grading periods or textbook orders. But an unexpected call from a parent or a student who needs your attention can throw plans into disarray. Certain cadences, like the ends of quarters or semesters, will be predictably hard. Others will take you by surprise.

Though it's problematic to generalize too much, it seems safe to say that while any given teacher's job can be stressful, even crisis-driven, the calendar tends to place boundaries on just how frenzied things can get. One of the most deeply satisfying aspects of a teaching career is that every June you really do close the books on a school year. Inevitably there are loose ends — the project that needs to be suspended until the fall; the student who needs, for good reasons or bad, a grade of incomplete. Endings can be delayed by postmortem meetings or cleanups; beginnings can commence early for setting things up. But summer always has more or less discrete boundaries. Though administrators are tethered to their posts, faculties eventually join students in collective flight from a campus before June is over, sometimes not returning for months.

Summers are complicated. There are some teachers — probably a relatively small minority — who actually take the whole thing off. Others manage to get in something (or maybe a few short somethings) at different points over the summer, whether standard getaways to nearby beaches or exotic destinations involving long-distance travel. By and large, however, summer is a time when teachers supplement their incomes with additional jobs, like teaching minicourses or camp counseling. Summer is also a time when foundations are laid for new courses or curricula, with or without institutional support.

Summer is often cited by teacher and nonteacher alike as the single most attractive perk of the profession. ("What are the three best things about being a teacher? June, July, and August.") Every September I hear my colleagues say they had a great summer and lament that it went by so fast. I'll confess, though, that I've always found summers problematic. Maybe it's because I endured a couple of searingly boring ones in my adolescence, summers that made me feel like an isolated outsider long after the objective facts of my life changed for the better. Though my salary is annual, I also find summers tough financially: almost anything fun costs money, and unless you have a cash bump to fill the free time, you feel pinched. I'm also typically anxious to have something to show for my summer workwise, to complete a project that would be otherwise difficult to start or finish during the school year. I'm not saying I don't enjoy my summers. But there's often an undercurrent of anxiety, even dread, to them that has me counting days and very glad when they're over. I doubt my experience is widespread. I also doubt I'm alone in this regard.

The academic school year is the largest unit of measure of the concentric circles that shape a teacher's career. Some might cite the four-year cycle that marks the entrance or exit of a cohort of kids into and out of an institution, but since most teachers teach only a fraction (admittedly in some cases a large one) of any graduating class, the concentric circles begin to lose their shape once you get beyond individual years.

Indeed, one of the secrets of a long-term teaching life is its somewhat formless quality. We'd *like* to think that each year is its own little drama, but in fact years have a tendency to run together. While the sensitivities of our students are vividly, even jaggedly, clear when *they're* in high school, graduating classes start to become indistinguishable to faculties. Change can be subtle to the point of imperceptible; we tend to answer a question about when something happened in terms of whether it was before or after the middle school was built or colleague X retired. We pretend a particular class or student is special, and sometimes they are, but usually it's hard to remember what year it was that this one or that one graduated. This static feeling in a teaching life can be one of the most dismaying things about it, and one reason why the profession has relatively little prestige: it's a treadmill, not a ladder. But it also has its satisfactions, among them a sense of timelessness — for a while you actually believe that you're part of the very soul of a place — and a sense of genteel stability that's hard to match in any other line of work.

All this said, a linear dimension of time is never altogether absent, and as the years pass it becomes increasingly prominent in a teacher's consciousness. Here I'll cite the familiar truism about how for a teacher the kids never get any older even though *you* always do. Such musings are likely to result in a dull ache. At the start of a teaching career you are probably not even twice the age of your students. Gradually but inexorably the multiple grows from two to three to four and beyond. The collective perception your students have of you imperceptibly changes. At the start, some of them may think of you as virtually one of them, and this helps you to relate to them and to translate ideas into a shared frame of reference. (If *you* think of your students as your peers, though, sticky situations can easily arise.) Then you become more of a parental, and eventually even a grandparental, figure. This has its advantages, too. But effectiveness on the job may require you to make some (perhaps surreptitious) effort to maintain a little cultural currency with their music or fads, not so much because anybody believes you're actually cool anymore, but rather because the effort demonstrates that you care about them — it's a gesture of reciprocity. In my own case this means peppering my tests with silly extra-credit questions about the celebrity of the moment. Such gestures can stretch your sense of relevance in a school community for a while.

But maintaining this sense of currency can be hard. It's hard because you may well find it difficult to take their culture seriously (you've heard it all before), and because their innocence — which you sometimes experience as thoughtlessness — can be tiresome. Actually, merely coexisting with children day after day can make you feel foolish at times. On the one hand, you find yourself envying their health, smarts, and beauty, which you either never had or know you're soon going to lose (if you haven't already). On the other, you can find yourself feeling a little infantilized compared to friends and family who spend their days among adults with adult concerns. Our society has long considered children priceless and professed to honor those who attend to them. But the actual lack of status in the job can be harder to take the older you get, especially given the absence of the career ladder that many other professions have. A dreaded question hovers over cocktail parties and reunions: "Still teaching, Horace?"

In the end, the best refuge from all of this is to shift one's gaze from linear time back to circular time. There's an eternal now to be savored in the rhythms of the profession in the form of students who care about neither where you were or where you'll be and who want to work with you where you are. Stay with the current.

⁂

"She's a sweetheart, isn't she?" Hank Langone says to me as we watch Kendra put her coat on to head home from the holiday party. Hank is the chair of the math department and something of a school legend for his quick wit as well as his ability to make math seem easy—well, eas*ier*, anyway.

"Lovely," I reply. I don't think we're actually ogling Kendra, but the idea of two middle-aged white guys watching a younger black woman without her knowledge makes me feel a little uneasy.

"She was a real catch," Hank continues, clearly not on my wavelength. "Had to convince Hannah to do some creative accounting with her experience in order to boost her starting salary. African American math teachers are hard to come by. She had three offers. Sidwell Friends and Milton matched us, but she wanted to be in New York. Her partner works in admissions at Brearley."

I nod, getting the feeling that I'm really just a distant chorus for Hank's internal reverie.

"I'm hoping she'll be my legacy. That after I leave people will say, 'He's the guy who brought Kendra Parks here.'"

"I think you're selling yourself a little short, Hank."

He looks at me. "This isn't false modesty. I know I'm good. I also know I'm just passing through. A year after I'm gone I'll be a memory to the students here. Two years, a rumor. Four years, I'm erased entirely. Seen it happen. Over and over." Hank takes a swig of beer. I wonder how many he's had. (I'm always a little amazed that alcohol gets served at this school function.) "That's just the way it is," he says, his voice a mixture of matter-of-factness and resignation. "Iron law of history—you should know, right?"

"I guess."

There's a lull. I think about leaving. Then Hank speaks up again in a quickening voice: "Hey, Horace, you like Elvis Costello?"

"Sure. Saw him live once."

"You know that song 'Girls Talk'?"

"Yeah. Nick Lowe recorded it, right?"

"Yeah, but I like Elvis's version better. Song has my favorite line of all time."

"What's that?"

Hank sings: "You may not be an old-fashioned girl / but you're gonna get dated." He takes another swig. "Old Elvis—or maybe I should say young Elvis, or the other Elvis—was right. Even our dear friend Kendra. Kinda breaks my heart to think that even she will be old one day."

"Gee, Hank, thanks so much for these cheery holiday sentiments."

Hank laughs—a hearty laugh that almost sounds incongruous. He punches me on the arm. "Shit, Horace, even white guys can sing the blues, no?" He puts his beer down on a crowded table. "Anyway, guess I should be going, too." He heads over to the coat rack and finds his. As he hoists his shoulders into the arms of his coat I say, "If I don't see you, happy holidays, Hank."

He looks up from buttoning his coat. "Happy hol — awww, fuck it. Merry Christmas, Horace. Right? He beams at me. "Merry fucking Christmas. That's where we are. Am I not right, my friend?"

I hoist an imaginary glass. "You are. Merry fucking Christmas, Hank. God rest you merry gentleman." On the drive home I listen to *The Best of Elvis Costello*, which I have on my phone. Elvis is singing about wanting to bite the hand that feeds him. His rage cheers me greatly.

SUBJECT MATTERS

Thursday afternoon, 12:35. I take the tray bearing soup, salad, a piece of apple pie, and a glass of water to the table currently occupied by my colleagues Denise Richardson and Troy Ricci. Denise is the doyenne of the English department; Troy is the longtime chair of visual arts.

"Ah, Horace," Troy says, "I was hoping you could help me talk some sense into Denise here."

"Not likely," I say, sitting down and reaching for the salt and pepper.

"Oh no?" Denise asks, taking faux umbrage. "Am I really that far beyond redemption, Horace?"

"No, no, Denise. I mean that I hardly make enough sense to myself, never mind anyone else."

Troy pushes the tray with the remains of his lunch a few inches forward. "I was just telling her about the first meeting of the schedule task force that I attended yesterday. I pitched an idea I have about switching from a semester model to a trimester model."

I had heard about this. In fact, Troy himself had told me. He's speaking as if he hadn't, probably because he knows I like the idea and I can come off as a fair-minded listener who embraces the proposal upon learning of it for the first time. That's fine with me. I like jousting with Denise.

I nod slowly as if I were taking this in. "I like it."

Denise rolls her eyes. "C'mon, Horace. You're not serious."

"Sure I am. I'm assuming this is mostly a matter of electives, right, Troy? Something like tenth-grade chemistry can be a three-trimester sequence."

Troy gestures with his hand to Denise: "Exactly."

She exhales in exasperation. "Our most interesting courses are the electives. How am I going to teach my Dostoevsky class in a trimester? You can barely finish a novel in that amount of time!" Denise is legendary for the snail's pace with which her classes digest fiction, often dedicating a whole period to a single paragraph. But she's good at what she does, and her palpable love for literature — and her students — has made her one of the most popular teachers at the school.

"So you do short stories instead." I take a stab at my salad.

"Come *on*, Horace. Are you telling me that you don't get it?"

"Get what?" I roll a green olive in some dressing.

"That learning this stuff requires continuity and context! You can't rush through it in a few weeks."

"Sure you can."

"No you can't. The students will have no sense of how the work relates to a bigger picture. They won't be able to understand what they read."

This puzzles me. Given her penchant for close reading of texts, I'm surprised Denise is putting so much emphasis on context. I'm tempted to point this out, though the truth is I don't really know what she does on any given day. Maybe she goes so slowly precisely because she's giving so much background. So I ask, "Why can't they appreciate the work on its own terms?"

"Because they won't understand what they're reading! That's our job: to help create a good reading experience."

Troy jumps in. "But why does that have to be understood solely in literary terms? Doesn't it count, for example, if a kid is learning about Russian history at the same time he's taking the Dostoevsky course? Or taking the Legal Eagles electives alongside reading *Crime and Punishment*?"

Denise takes a drink of soda, probably to slow herself down. "In theory, it counts. But if you've got a trimester system, that means students are taking many more courses each year. Their whole education experience becomes a blender. They're already doing too much."

"Which is why," Troy says, with a trace of impatience in his voice, "I'm also proposing a cap on how many courses a student can take. Just four at a time. That will allow them to concentrate on what they're really doing."

"Great. So that means they can skip English entirely for stretches at a time."

"Jesus, Denise. How about sharing the love a little?" Troy seems genuinely annoyed now. "Nobody debates the importance of English. Some of us aren't so lucky. If a kid has a trimester without poetry, they'll make it up later. This will allow them more of a chance to try other things. A trimester system gives them a way of avoiding scheduling conflicts and can keep them from getting overwhelmed."

I'm about to point out to Troy that the state mandates four years of English. But Denise is shaking her head, and I'm curious to hear how she's going to respond. "All I'm saying is that choppiness isn't good for anybody." She's trying to sound conciliatory. But it's not coming out that way.

"But choppiness is what we have *now*, Denise. You're just insulated from it. Except that you're not. Or at least your students are not. You think they're actually *reading* all that Dostoevsky while they shuttle between your class, physics, intensive Spanish, and the soccer team?"

"So what I am supposed to do? Give up?"

"I think what Troy means," I say soothingly, "is that we need to pull our heads out of the sand. Maybe a trimester isn't the best solution, though I must say I think it has a lot to recommend it. But everybody feels like what they do is important. And in the process, the kids are suffering from intellectual, and even physical, whiplash."

Denise is arranging the dishes on her tray as a prelude to making an exit. "It's a problem, I know." She sounds more measured now. "But the solution will not be a matter of shuffling the scheduling deck. Students have to understand that they need to make choices—to live is to choose. Only by choosing can you begin to value what you have." Then she fixes her gaze on me. "Horace, you know we live in an anti-intellectual culture. You *know* that. If *you* won't stand up for the life of the mind, it would sadden me greatly." She stands up with her tray and then leans over, kissing the top of my head. "But you're not going to do that, are you." She walks away. I'm flattered by her affection but suspect I'm unworthy of it.

Troy is shaking his head, chuckling. "You see what we're up against. The foreign language and math departments aren't going to go for this, either. I should probably just give up."

"Hang in there, Troy," I say as he leaves. "It's a good idea. And I'm with you on this." But as I watch a kid to my left spectacularly lose control of his tray amid mock applause, I wonder: am I?

⁂

Whatever teachers may have in common—however much that identity transcends where or whom you're teaching—every teacher is finally a teacher of *something*: a math teacher, a science teacher, a learning specialist, and so on. In elementary schools, expertise tends to be defined in terms of grade level, though even there one will find, sometimes literally, degrees of specialization ("I hold a master's in early childhood education"). To be sure, there's often a measure of flexibility in one's training—a physics teacher who's prepared to handle a math course, say, or a second-grade teacher who makes the move to fifth. But while teachers are trained in different ways with different amounts of depth in particular subject areas, establishing a claim as a professional educator involves credentialing in one or more specific academic disciplines.

I am stating, even belaboring, the obvious. As is so often true in our everyday lives, however, the obvious can be surprisingly easy to lose sight of amid other considerations. The life of the mind is relatively unimportant to most students, but it can also be relatively unimportant to faculty, though for different reasons. Students are often caught up in their social lives and the rituals of their school culture, choosing not to think about their classes for significant chunks of time. Teachers have their diversions too, but much of what they're paid to do — much of what administrators expect of them — has nothing to do with academic concerns, their own or anyone else's. These other responsibilities range from routine housekeeping, like taking attendance, to graver obligations, like reporting child abuse. Most school communities (a term I use here to encompass faculty, administration, staff, and parents) affirm the concept of educating "the whole child," which, ambiguities and limits aside, includes things like paying attention to the socialization of students, providing some degree of ethical instruction and modeling, and playing a constructive role for students who find themselves in psychological or other kinds of distress. This hidden curriculum, as it's sometimes called, is indeed an element of schooling. But it's not an *academic* part of schooling.

Old-time journalists used the term *news hole* to refer to the amount of time (in television or radio) or space (in newspapers or magazines) that actually exists for stories after one takes into account advertising, promos, standard items like weather maps, and the like. One can similarly speak of a "curriculum hole," meaning the time for instruction that's left after lunch, recess, assemblies, meetings, and other segments that constitute a school day are factored in. Sometimes — especially when I'm feeling unprepared for a class — I become aware that the curriculum hole is not trivial: you really do have to fill chunks of time that can seem cavernous if you don't know what you're talking about. And while high-minded progressives or desperate improvisers can rightly claim that class time can and should be used for students to engage with each other and take charge of their own learning, a class can't function well unless there's someone who's at least an editor, if not an instructor with a plan.

Fortunately, teachers aren't blank slates. They usually come to the classroom with years of experience in the subject at hand. I don't want to make too much of this: the quality of a teacher's training isn't always good; teachers are often to asked to teach well outside of their comfort zones; complacency and boredom always hover around the veteran who rests on laurels. Still, there's usually a kernel of ability — and, one hopes, passion — available if a teacher can connect (or reconnect) with it.

I sometimes think of a teacher's relationship to a subject as akin to a marriage. It may begin with casual acquaintance, brokered by family, friends, or an appealing teacher. An infatuation follows as the budding educator pursues the subject in venues beyond school. A major or degree in a field is a statement of commitment, and getting a teaching job weds one to a subject. Occasionally a teacher will leave one discipline for another; there are also cases of academic polygamy across disciplines or departments (which is tolerated, though not always comfortable from the standpoint of administrative or faculty politics). But the understanding is that bona fide devotion to a specific field of knowledge will be part of the equation as long as the teacher remains in the profession.

Perhaps the more relevant aspect of the marital analogy has to do with a teacher's relationship with a subject over time. The challenge as the years pass involves keeping one's passion alive. Part of the difficulty, as I've already suggested, is that so many other aspects of school life compete for a teacher's attention. But one can also get restless with a subject, particularly after teaching the same material repeatedly. A little experimentation may help — if one has the energy to stretch. Summers can also help recharge intellectual batteries.

My own relationship with my chosen discipline of history illustrates these dynamics, notwithstanding its peculiarities. I loved history as a child. But when it came time to go to college, I majored in English (I never actually took a course in US history). And my graduate work, which I began two years after getting my bachelor's degree in 1985, was in the interdisciplinary field of American civilization. Still, early on in my studies I gravitated toward history again.

It's hard to explain how this happened. At no point in my undergraduate or graduate years did I ever make a conscious choice for history. And yet a desire to contextualize any new information I imbibed became central. To know when that book was written; what else was going on when that album was released; what ideas preceded or followed those of a particular thinker: such questions were always foremost in my thinking. I did have in interest in ideas for their own sake, and I savored aesthetic experiences of images and words. But time became the primary lens through which I saw the wider world.

I don't think we choose such things; they're a matter of temperament and innate orientation. Some of us sense, and are drawn to, the elegance of numbers. Others marvel at the living things with which we share the earth. (Perhaps, unlike me, they would not call them "things.") I've experienced people like that, and as I do I'm aware that while I can appreciate their interests, I'm simply not enchanted by the same phenomena that they are. But through some combination of intellect and persuasion I can begin to acquire an interest in, and understanding of, numbers and creatures I otherwise would not have had. A great teacher will provoke students to develop their innate abilities, offer positive reinforcement, and generate a positive feedback loop. But such generativity is not easy to predict or control — nor is it entirely conscious.

I chalk up my interest in American history to narcissism: I wanted to know where I came from. From a very early point — certainly it was not something I picked up as part of my formal education — I had a powerful perception of being born at the end of an era of national confidence and security. My schooling helped me understand the contours of that confidence and security, and the price it exacted on others. And yet even as I acknowledge the failures of my native country, the crimes that thread through its very origins, I cannot relinquish my attachment. Here I'm reminded of the words of F. Scott Fitzgerald. "I look out at it and I think it is the most beautiful history in the world," he said of American history at the end of his life. "It is the history of all aspiration — not just the American dream but the human dream and if I came at the end of it that too is a place in the line of the pioneers."[1] The greatest compliment I've ever received as a teacher came from a student in a graduation speech who paid tribute to "Mr. Dewey, who made us love history almost as much as he does."

Part of what it means to be educated, however, involves disciplining this love, subjecting it to the scrutiny and rigor of systematic study. The most pivotal part of my graduate training involved spending eighteen months reading the most important scholarship in nineteenth-century US social, political and intellectual history. I summarized each of the dozens of books I read on 5×8-inch index cards, which I stored in a box that remains in my desk to this day. At the end of the process, when I passed a comprehensive oral exam administered by my professors, I joked that I was driving around a 1989 model of US history: the scholarship I'd digested was a product of its moment, and it would continue to shape my consciousness long after I finished my schooling, and long after new scholarship was being produced.

Naturally, I hoped that in the years that followed I would stay up to date by reading new historical writing. And to a great degree I have. But of course it's been impossible to keep up with all of it. Actually, as time has passed I've become increasingly interested in aspects of US history that were not the focus of my training. In recent years I've read a lot of colonial US history and even began to dabble in subjects like ancient Greece and Rome. I've savored this reading as an avowed amateur, but it has provided a layer of seasoning to my standard repertoire (such as in my attempts to compare the Roman and American republics in discussions of the Constitution) and efforts to incorporate fresh elements in my classes (like adding a unit on Julius Caesar in a biography course that also included units on Frederick Douglass and Elvis Presley).

Nowadays, the chief challenge I face isn't so much the need to juggle lots of balls in my job and my personal life. Instead, it's been a struggle to maintain my memory and find room for storage in what feels like a full mental hard drive. (Even my metaphors are old-fashioned: I don't think in terms of clouds of storage.) I was chagrined to recently buy, read, and annotate Frances Fitzgerald's 1982 study of US history textbooks, *America Revised*, only to discover as I was shelving it not only that I already owned another copy but that I had read and annotated it five years earlier. The foundation of my reading habit had always been a deep confidence in self-improvement, a serene assurance that even the most boring books were nevertheless contributing to an edifice of knowledge that reinforced my mental powers. I've lost that faith. It's been hard.

But I haven't lost *all* faith. I still like to read, but I'm a little pickier now, because I want the experience of reading to be more satisfying—I'm less interested in information for its own sake. I've always had a strong appetite for fiction, especially historical fiction, but it has strengthened considerably, as has my interest in film and television with historical settings. I'm now more focused mining history to deepen aesthetic and emotional experience.

To some extent, I am taking this focus with me into the classroom. I feel like I've lived long enough to become a skeptic about ideology (reality is more complicated than political theory allows) and epistemology (I like to tell my students that life is an existential condition marked by insufficient information). History—and, I strongly suspect, science, math, and other subjects—is really a matter of making sense of the little you do know, given the large amount that you don't.

So I feel like I'm shrinking, though in my more hopeful moments I like to think of myself as becoming leaner. I don't think the mental limits I'm experiencing are obvious to my students yet; I hope they won't be for a while. Of course the biggest danger is that I'll fail to recognize how diminished I actually am. I hope I'll be able to afford, in the broadest sense of that term, to step aside when the time comes.

But even at my most expansive, what I've had to offer my students, academically speaking, has always been finite. My smartest students have been those who have been able to size me up, figure out what I have to offer in terms of knowledge or the ability to foster skills, and move on. I want to be helpful to them as an authority figure, and I like to be liked. But I also want to be experienced, and remembered, as a man who actually knew some things about a particular discipline and who leveraged that knowledge to enhance his students' understanding of the world. The subject matters.

🐜🐌🐜

A perfect spring morning—impossibly blue cloudless sky, crystalline air, enough of a chill to promise no sticky classroom this afternoon. As I head from the parking lot to the back door of the library, I see biology teacher Tommy Horowitz, as I often do in the morning, conversing with his seven year-old daughter Isabel before he takes her over to the elementary school on the other side of campus. Some days Tommy and Isabel are hunched over a plant. Other days they're looking up at a tree or a bird. (Decades from now, this child will be reliving these moments. I see a faint smile on the face of an aging woman.) Today, though, they appear to have wandered into the realm of geology: they're standing near two large rectangular rocks that are about four feet wide and two feet deep. A landscaping crew, not yet on the job, is in the process of creating an outdoor classroom. These slabs look like they'll function as benches.

Tommy beckons me over. "Look at this," he says, pointing to the rocks on the ground, which I can see have a chalky gray color and texture. I see the imprint of what appear to be elongated clam shells. I guess these are what you'd call fossils.

"How old do you think they are?" Tommy asks me, pointing to a specific shell. I can see the rock in question is mottled with them.

I look up at the administration building through some trees. It's built in a Tudor style, though of course centuries later and an ocean away from where the Tudors held dominion. This campus was erected in 1928. I'm guessing we're standing in what was once swampland. "I dunno—a hundred years?"

"I'm thinking a hundred million years," Tommy replies. "It might be older. This species is extinct." There's no element of gotcha here; he's not the faintest bit amused by how far off I am. His excitement, palpable as a child's, is entirely devoted to observing this sign of life. Isabel, who has been staring at me neutrally—what on earth is this child thinking?—shifts her gaze back to the rocks. Tommy has resumed directing his comments to her, pointing out features in the marbled stone, tracing lines as if they were text.

I still think a trimester system is the way for us to go, though I fear Troy's despair at how hard it will be to implement is all too justified. But in the end, whatever the schedule, there's no substitute for the Tommys and Denises whose commitment to their subject is finally not rational. We teach what we love in the hope that we can reproduce it.

PROGRESSIVE FAITH

I write five words on the whiteboard five times, each time underlining a different word:

<u>All</u> men are created equal.
All <u>men</u> are created equal.
All men <u>are</u> created equal.
All men are <u>created</u> equal.
All men are created <u>equal</u>.

"So, kids, are *any* of these statements true?" I ask, turning around to face the class. "I mean, what a crock of bull, right? How could Jefferson — himself a slave owner — possibly be serious?"

A few wry smiles. Some of them have apparently asked themselves this question before.

"I *love* that line!" Vanessa Thompson, ever the contrarian in her vintage Sex Pistols T-shirt. (Does she have even the vaguest idea about who the Sex Pistols were? Last year I asked Emma Lopez, who was wearing a Lynyrd Skynyrd T-shirt, if she was a fan. She said she had no idea — the shirt was Taylor Hutchinson's and she had borrowed it.) But Vanessa's been too busy chatting with Janey Orlov to be much of a presence today.

"Doesn't matter whether they believe it," says Eduardo Salinas. "It's propaganda."

I try to mask my surprise. This is the first time I've heard from Eduardo since I picked him up in this rotation of my humanities class, which began just last week. I want to kindle the flame without smothering him.

"You think they're lying?"

"Dunno," he replies. "Maybe."

"You called this 'propaganda.' What do you mean by that?"

"I mean they're trying to persuade people."

"Can propaganda be true?"

"I guess."

"Do you think they were trying to persuade themselves?"

Eduardo shrugs. I can't tell whether he's expressing skepticism or a desire to be let off the hook.

"I think they did believe it," Zoe Leoni says without raising her hand. "I mean, you kind of *have* to believe it if you're going to stick your neck out like that." I like the psychological acuity Zoe shows here.

"You say 'they.' Do 'they' all think the same way?"

"No, probably not. But I don't think they really have any choice. They're desperate, right? Didn't you say yesterday that there's like this big invasion the British are planning?"

"Right. They've already landed on Long Island. They're headed for Manhattan even as the Declaration of Independence is being written."

"So of *course* they're going to talk about life, liberty, and the pursuit of happiness. So it sounds like they're the good guys."

"But how do they think they can get away with it?"

"It was a bunch of rich white guys who wanted other people to help them keep their slaves," Derek Simonson, who sits next to Eduardo, blurts out with an edge of impatience in his voice. Wonder of wonders: two silent types in one day.

"Well, now, that's a fascinating theory," I say, more eager to encourage him than to pursue the angle of ideological difference between the revolutionaries. "A big part of the Declaration was designed to attract foreign support, especially from the French. But here's what I wonder, Derek: is this really the best language to use in order to do something like that? Let's assume you're right: these guys are essentially a bunch of frauds, and people then could see through them then just like you are now. I'm reminded of the famous writer Samuel Johnson's response to the colonists: 'How is it that we hear the loudest yelps for liberty from the drivers of negroes?' So why do you think *they* think a lot of life, liberty, and happiness talk is really going to convince anybody?"

Derek does not seem inclined to answer my question, but Jiian Cheng raises his hand, and I acknowledge him. "I don't think they really have any choice. I mean, you gotta start somewhere."

Lara Lynn wants to weigh in, and I nod to her. "I agree. Jiian's right. It's an important first step."

"A step towards what?"

"Freedom. Independence. All that stuff."

"Well, OK." I point at the whiteboard. "But this says 'all men are created equal.'"

Lara hesitates. Then: "Yeah, that too."

"So freedom and equality go together? How does this work — first we get the freedom, then we do equality?"

She's lost. "Yeah, kinda."

I shift my gaze from Lara and make a puzzled expression to the class generally. "I don't get it, kids. What does freedom have to do with equality? Are they the same thing?"

What I regard as a fruitful line of discussion is disrupted by Wilhelmina (aka Willie) Sperry, who has already emerged as one of my favorite kids, maybe of all time. I often see Willie walking the hallways, weighed down by a backpack that looks like it's crushing her and bearing a grim expression, in marked contrast to the animated child who's most fully alive in the classroom. In other words, a girl after my own heart. Not pretty, really — red-haired and a little scrawny — but Willie has a warm personality that has always made her appealing, at least to adults and what seems to be a small circle of friends. But will the boys see it? Willie, who has been silently following today's conversation with her usual intensity, chooses this moment to raise her hand. "They're hypocrites," she says. "The king simply has to go after them. If they're allowed to get away with this, it would set a bad example. They've insulted him . . ."

I begin to lose track of what Willie is saying. For one thing, it seems tangential: what does the king have to do with what we've been talking about? For another, I realize I'm hungry. And yet I marvel at how fully immersed Willie is in this discourse. Even Janey Orlov has noticed. Not approvingly.

I cut her off. "I'm not sure we need to shed any tears for George III, Willie. If there's anyone in the world who can brush off some punk critics, surely it's him. But I tell you who I am worried about," I say, pausing for effect. "The king of Spain." I put my hand on my chin and narrow my eyes. "I mean, here's a guy who's going to be losing sleep at night."

"Who *is* the king of Spain?" Willie asks, genuinely curious.

"I dunno," I reply, not changing my expression. "Carlos the Twenty-something. They were all called Carlos back then." The class breaks into laughter.

"See, here's the problem," I say when it subsides. "There's *nothing* old Carlos would like more than to stick it to Britain. He wants it so badly he can almost taste it. The problem is that if he and his Bourbon cousin Louis XVI enter an American war against Britain on the side of a group of rebels who have issued this revolutionary manifesto, then his own subjects in places like Mexico and Peru might actually begin to take some of the nonsense in that manifesto seriously. And that would be a real mess."

"So what does he do?" This from Vanessa, who's back among us. My, my, I *am* on a roll today.

"Well, ultimately he takes the plunge — he joins France and declares war on Britain. Which in a way is great: he's got France's back, which allows the French to send a naval force to the decisive Battle of Yorktown, and Spain picks up a lot of real estate in Florida. But his fears prove justified, because within a generation all hell breaks loose in Central and South America. Eventually the Mexicos and Perus of the world declare their own independence. The king of France, who tended not to worry as much, ends up literally losing his head in the name of abstract ideals like freedom and equality — which, I'll point out in passing, we're still lumping together as if they're two sides of the same coin. We can't blame all of this on the Declaration of Independence, of course. But it certainly didn't help matters if you're the king of Spain.

"Which," I continue, after a pause, "is another way of saying that you're right, Eduardo and Derek. The Declaration of Independence *was* a piece of propaganda by a bunch of rich white guys who were desperate enough to say whatever they thought might work at that particular moment. The problem was that in so doing they let a genie out of a bottle, because some people, despite much evidence to the contrary, actually began to believe what the Declaration said — or, maybe more accurately, they *acted* as if they believed what the Declaration said. 'Acted' in the sense that they pretended, and 'acted' also in the sense that they ended up doing things that they might not have done had there been no Declaration of Independence. That genie ended up doing a whole lot of mischief all over the world."

"Still does," Willie says with a smile.

"You think so?"

"Yes."

"Really?"

"Yes." Willie is firm. So smart, so innocent. Eduardo is packing up his books: the signal that my time is up. Derek is looking, inscrutably, at Willie. Oh, dear girl.

"How about that," I say. "You think so too, Zoe? You think Willie is right?"

She nods noncommittally.

"Well, then, I guess we've figured this all out. See you tomorrow."

People of all temperaments and ideological persuasions become teachers, but the nature of the job as it's currently constituted makes them instinctive progressives. I should add that I'm using the term in multiple senses — some of which I don't wholeheartedly embrace — but their valences are powerful and should be recognized, even if they're not dominant in the US education system in particular or American society generally.

In its most specific educational usage, the word *progressive* refers to a pedagogical philosophy that took root in the late nineteenth century and has in various iterations persisted to this day. At its core it emphasizes process (like discussion) over product (like test scores); subjective experience over objective truth; learning by doing rather than having information delivered. As a movement, progressive education in this country probably peaked in the 1930s, and it has largely persisted as an alternative educational subculture in the decades since.

That said, important elements of the progressive ethos have long been absorbed as common sense even in schools that do not consider themselves progressive. They may emphasize traditional values, basic skills, and mastery of content. But they will hardly disparage — indeed, they will likely explicitly uphold — critical thinking, diversity of thought and experience, and pragmatic problem solving, all of which are hallmarks of progressive education. Virtually no educators will claim that lecturing is the best means of delivering instruction, even when teacher-centered information delivery is in fact their primary approach. Ironically, one of the major problems for the contemporary progressive education movement is that many of its core ideas are now taken for granted, even when they conflict with others. Parents and educators insist on growth *and* rigor, or diversity *and* continuity, whether or not they're simultaneously achievable.

The second way teachers tend to be progressive is more generally political. In school systems of all sizes, where different constituencies jockey for maximum room to maneuver, teachers are the inheritors of the Progressive tradition — note the capital *P* to indicate the movement in US electoral politics that spanned roughly 1890 to 1920. It's important to add, however, that there was a curious bifurcation in the Progressive movement that it never entirely resolved. On the one hand, early Progressives were locally based, experimental, and highly empirical in their approach to social reform (not just in schools but also in business regulation, municipal services, and electoral reform, among other initiatives). They were very much bottom-up. On the other hand, Progressives were also — and this became increasingly apparent as the movement gained momentum in the second decade of the twentieth century, when it dominated the nation's political life in both major parties — great centralizers of power, as long as it was concentrated in the hands of independent experts who professed to act in the name of the common

good. If the settlement house worker Jane Addams personi-
fied the first strand of Progressivism, Theodore Roosevelt was
the epitome of the second. And by the time of Roosevelt's
successor, Woodrow Wilson, there were growing questions
about whether experts really could be trusted to act on the
common good — Wilson, who held a PhD in political science,
was notoriously high-handed in his foreign policy, for example — and whether they really knew as much as they thought
they did. Though Progressives and their contemporary heirs
have always thought of themselves of champions of The People, their skeptics have always regarded them, not without
reason, as elitists insufferably blind to their own arrogance.

Whether or not they identify as latter-day inheritors of the
old Progressive tradition, most teachers in their day-to-day
lives embrace the Progressivism of the localized Jane Addams
variety. In contrast to administrators or politicians who want
to impose their ideas for reform from the top down, teachers
see themselves working with the facts on the ground: particular children in a specific time and place responding to
circumstances that may or may not correspond to a reform
template. To at least some extent, this is a matter of self-
interest: workers in many occupations tend to insist on the
necessity of discretion to perform their job well. But teachers aren't the only ones who make this case for their role in
the classroom; a long tradition of reformers, some of them
in positions of administrative authority, have embraced the
principle of teacher autonomy, even if this has always been a
minority view in policy-making circles.

The third and most decisive way in which teachers tend to
be progressive is what might be termed temperamental. In a
literal sense, to be a progressive is to believe in progress, and
anyone who's in the business of educating children and does
not believe in progress is probably in the wrong line of work.

In this realm, too, the word has multiple meanings.

The most fundamental, of course, is at the level of the individual child. Teachers must act as if—and at least try to believe that—every student is capable of improving. This uniform principle gets affirmed in highly variable ways. A good teacher will assess where a student is and identify an attainable goal, and in a good teacher's assessment of student work, the distance that student travels will matter at least as much as the objective quality of the work. The essence of fairness in this context means taking differences into account, honoring the struggle more than any effortlessly achieved excellence. This is an admittedly tricky matter, inherently subjective in nature. But it's a standard worth pursuing. Virtually all students *do* make progress, variously understood, over the course of their academic careers. The school or instructional climate will never entirely account for it, though such factors (among them a child's teacher) really can matter.

This progressive principle also applies to the craft of teaching itself. As anyone who's done it for any length of time will agree, you get better at it as you go along. Improvement can come via formal professional development, acquiring more knowledge from casual reading, or simply mastering a curriculum by repeatedly teaching it. There is certainly something to be said for the vitality of a new teacher, whose receptiveness to experience and willingness to shoulder often onerous demands (like teaching unfamiliar material) should not be underestimated as a source of institutional vitality. And there's no question that dead wood—which is to say teachers who have given up trying to grow—is a problem at virtually every school. But the seasoned veteran teacher is an asset any successful school will have in abundance.

The most profound way in which teachers are temperamentally progressive is generational: they believe in the future, a faith grounded in their engagement with the children who will take their place as adults. Strictly speaking, having desire and ability to work with young people don't necessarily mean you think the future will be better than the past. (I don't, for reasons I'll explain shortly.) But unless you're animated by *some* sense of hope about tomorrow, teaching becomes an exercise in grim fatalism, no doubt a contributing factor in dead wood syndrome.

Perhaps more than teachers elsewhere, American teachers have a particular attachment to seeing their work as part of a larger national drama. For much of the nineteenth century, the dominant strain of historical interpretation in Great Britain and the United States was the so-called Whig school, which emphasized the degree to which history was a story of progress — moral no less than scientific — embodied in the white, Anglo-Saxon, and Protestant politicians who emphasized the importance of liberty (notably the liberty of American colonists in their revolutionary struggle for independence, whose supporters in England were known as Whigs). The Whig interpretation of history fell out of favor around the time of the First World War — events in the first half of the twentieth century discredited confident assumptions of progress — and is regarded as racist today. But the notion that American life has been one of gradual improvement remains an article of faith that continues to animate everyday life inside as well as outside of classrooms.

You can see this progressive sensibility in just about any US history textbook. If the Whig school cast its notion of progress in terms of white supremacy, these books instead depict a slow, irregular, but unmistakable march toward pluralistic egalitarianism. Particularly in early chapters, these books have a demographic emphasis. We're introduced to groups of people of African, European, and Native American origin, and the divisions and interplay between them. However subjugated they are at the hands of imperial Europeans, those shut out of power manage to maintain their dignity and their hope in the face of considerable adversity. Though they experience tragedy, even catastrophe, they manage collectively to live another day. They'll have their postcolonial moment, just as the United States has. History is destiny — of a hopeful kind. It's what we think students need.

But — and this was the point of that opening anecdote — this progressive version of US history is not something *I* tell my students. This is something *they* tell *me*. It's a logic they've absorbed into their bones long before they reach my classroom. I've done this "all men are created equal" exercise a bunch of times, and it always goes pretty much the same way. I'll usually get a student or two who says it really is nonsense. But inevitably one or two students will come forward and say that such a judgment is too harsh. I press them to explain, they may or may not flail in their attempt to do so, and a classmate or two (or three) will jump in. The gist of their riposte will be, in effect, that the Declaration of Independence was a kind of first draft of progressive history. First the white men were created equal. Then we remembered the ladies. Then the slaves got freed. And so on through gay marriage. That's our history. It may be short on facts. But it's long on vision — which, let's face it, is the most you can really hope for in a history course.

My problem is I'm not sure *I* really believe it. Yes: it is possible, desirable — right — to think of events like the ending of slavery, suffrage for women, the egalitarian achievements of the Progressive era, the New Deal, and the civil rights movement(s) as constituting an upward moral as well as material trajectory in American history. But if we stipulate that — and we put aside social hydraulics that seem to suggest gains for some people always mean losses for others (e.g., the decline of economic equality that has accompanied racial equality in the last four decades)—progress is not a permanent state. Republics and empires come and go: *that* seems to be the iron law of history. The arc of history is long, but it *is* an arc: what goes up must come down.

Unfortunately, this is not something I'm experiencing as an abstract proposition. Virtually every sentient American in the early twenty-first century is uncomfortably aware of a discourse of decline in our national life, particularly in the economic and political realm. Though (shockingly for anyone over thirty) events like 9/11, the Iraq War, and the financial crisis of 2008 are distant events for today's students, all have grown up in homes where recent history casts long shadows. Such events loom large in some students' overall perception of American history; other students seem less affected, either because they haven't fully absorbed their impact or because they imagine them as developments that are not really part of the historical record. Mostly, I think, reconciling recent events with their progressive vision of history requires living with cognitive dissonance in the form of cultural lag that's quite common to people in all times and places.

I don't directly challenge the historical progressivism of my students, other than to note at some point in the school year that visions of history come in many shapes: circles, spirals, straight lines, and inclines (I usually draw them for the visual learners). I don't particularly want to pass on my fatalism, partially because my instinctive skepticism makes me question my own certitude—events rarely happen in the way or at the pace we predict. But even if I did have certainty, I wouldn't push it on my students, because I can't see how it would do them any good. I don't want to puncture their confidence. Instead I hope to sharpen their understanding—here's where the facts and information come in, because they can help a good student get a particular version of the story straight—and send them on their way. In this regard I really *am* a progressive educator in that first pedagogical sense I talked about, the heir of a movement that emphasizes the plasticity of knowledge and the need for children to construct their own working models about the way the world works, but to do so in interaction with others.

And yet—and this is something I struggled with as a form of cognitive dissonance in my own life—I am not a progressive in the broadest, most historical sense of the term. There are days when I feel like I'm leading lambs to the slaughter, when I am fostering habits of thought and behavior that will be singularly unhelpful in a coming world that will not be like the one in which we are living. Sometimes I imagine that future world as one of chaos; other times it's one of stifling autocratic order. Either way, I imagine former students bitterly recalling the irrelevance, or worse, of what they learned in school.

So what keeps me going? My salvation is my ignorance: I don't know, I *can't* know, what will happen in the future. Call me an existentialist progressive: I labor in the faith—in the end, that's all it is—that something I do, something I say, something I ask my students to read will have some utility in their later lives. Some sliver that will be transubstantiated into an act of leadership—or, more simply, an act of decency—that will bring good into the life of that student and of the broader community. That's not much to count on, I know. But sometimes it's the counting that's the problem.

AMONG STUDENTS

NAME GAMES

"Excellent, Kim. The family structure—or maybe I should say the *lack* of family structure—in Virginia is indeed one of the distinguishing features between New England and the South in the seventeenth century. What are some other differences?"

Two hands go up. One is Sam Stevens, but he's already spoken too many times today. Uneasy about it, I gesture toward the other kid. "Go ahead—"

Shit! What's his name?

"—Yes. You. Go right ahead."

Fuck. This is embarrassing. He knows I don't know. And so does everybody else. Keep going—you've fumbled, but we're already on to the next play.

". . . and the Southern economy is about cotton," mystery kid is saying.

Bluff. "Yes, good, except that at this point the Chesapeake is really about tobacco, not cotton. Cotton won't come until much later, and further south and west. Yes, Cara? What do you think?"

Off she goes. Cara tends to unspool for a while before getting to the point. Normally this is exasperating. But now it gives me a chance to regroup.

It's week two of the new school year, and the ship whereon I can keep asking kids to identify themselves has already sailed. I've got most of them. But there are a couple (*Adam Kirby? Who the hell is he? And who's the other dirty-blond kid in the corner?*) who elude me. But I've *got* to get back in the saddle. Which is going to be hard, because I have no clue what Cara just said.

Phew. Wilhelmina's raising her hand. Port in a storm.

"What do you think, Willie?"

"Well, I just want to add on to what Adam said — "

Adam! Yes! So the other one looking at the clock must be Chris. I wonder which one of us is more desperate for class to end.

Silence. They're waiting. "Good, Willie."

I have no idea what she just said. Is that a smirk on Jack Al-tieri's face? He's such a prick. So was his brother. No way did he get into Duke on his own. C'mon now, Horace. Keep it together.

"So let me ask you this, gang. If you were a nineteen-year-old boy in 1625, where do you think you would rather go — colonial Williamsburg or colonial Plymouth?"

Finally. On track. Couple more comments and we'll wrap this up.

The only question now is whether I'll be able to keep Adam and Chris straight this time tomorrow morning. The odds, I think grimly, are 50-50. But as he goes out the door, I make a point of saying, "Take care, Adam." Maybe that will buy me a little goodwill? "Thanks," he says. *Schmuck*, he probably thinks.

🧍🧍🧍

There are many complex relationships in public life that blend the personal and professional in ways that defy easy description. But there's nothing quite like the dance of intimacy and formality between student and teacher. No teacher who connects emotionally with students will ever be considered a failure by them: *something* will be learned, and long remembered, whatever the teacher's competence in a given subject. But no teacher can be an effective educator without sustaining a discreet distance from students, emotional and otherwise. Finding the balance between the two is an unending life's work, a balance that different teachers calibrate in different ways, and one that often continues long after the official tie that connected student and teacher is severed — indeed sometimes even after a teacher retires.

Students always learn in multiple ways, even in school settings, and with the advent of online education the opportunities to do so have been expanding dramatically. But it remains a truism that students learn best when they work with a teacher who knows them (their first teachers, of course, are their parents). The chief way most schools economize is also among the most problematic: expanding class size. The bigger the class, the less likely that the teacher will know the students.

This of course raises the question of what it means to "know" a student. The most superficial answer is to be able to match a name and a face — which is not superficial at all as far as many students are concerned. One of my greatest sources of anxiety as a teacher is trying to get all my students' names down quickly at the start of every semester; another is trying to remember them after the class is over and after they've graduated. I have a palpable sense that they're going to hold it against me if I don't make this good-faith gesture of reciprocity and continuity: *if you can't remember my name, why should I remember anything you tell me?* It may be a misguided question, but it's there all the same, and no teacher who hopes to be effective can long ignore it. Alums are perhaps more forgiving than current students (something apparent at reunions, where the considerate ones say their names even if they're wearing name tags and allow you to say, "Of course I remember!").

A second level of knowing is similarly superficial and at the same time even more important: the impression you have of the student *as* a student. This is often a perception that takes shape even before you know his or her name: sharp or dull; active or passive; charming or abrasive. (I don't mean to link these adjective pairs; sometimes the ones you suspect are smartest hang back, for example.) Oftentimes you pick up such impressions unconsciously, taking your cue from body language, diction, the glaze of an eye. These sensory perceptions can prove quite accurate once you begin to see their work or talk with your colleagues about them. Then again they may not.

Right or wrong, your initial perceptions often prove significant — and not always in a good way. Once I get a sense of a kid as a B student, for example, it becomes harder — not impossible, but harder — for that kid to get an A, in part because I try to ration the As and am often looking for reasons to deny them in an effort to maintain a sense of standards: I want those As to actually mean something, if for no other reason than to allow a kid who gets one to feel she has earned something. I'm not usually *conscious* of being easier or tougher on kids I don't perceive as especially bright — or more lenient on kids I like for one reason or another — but on some level I know I must be. At the same time, my self-image requires me to show myself that I'm capable of revising my perceptions of a kid. So it is that we see through a glass darkly.

Knowledge of a student is also socially constructed, which is to say the product of perceptions of others which you have no way of verifying but you nevertheless absorb directly or indirectly. The locus of some reputations resides in the student body: he's a jock; she's a slut; they're geeks. Constructing and maintaining a persona is one of the most important tasks of childhood and (especially) adolescence, and one valuable indicator of intelligence is how effective a student is in modulating social equilibrium with peers and adults and toggling between them.

One's colleagues are also an important source of data about students. Some of this is in the official realm of report cards and other evaluations that are part of a student's scholastic record. More often information is anecdotal, varying greatly in its degree of legitimacy, even propriety. Some teachers, for example, are inveterate collectors of student romances, and the charm they find in them can be charming in its own right (or, alternatively, distasteful). There are times when gossip is genuinely helpful; it may lead you to see a student's behavior as part of a larger pattern or context, and in some cases it may lead you to make allowances (her parents are going through a divorce) or to take more forceful action (you mean he's done it to *you*, too?). The density of this informal database will vary depending on the size of the school, but given its richness, even intensity, schools sometimes feel like a repository of village living in an otherwise fragmented society. To be sure, such a climate may be suffocating, which is why many students are eager to get out and go far away. (We always end up sending a batch of kids to places like Cornell and the University of Michigan: bigger is better.) But it's no accident that most private high schools—which is to say schools where parents can pay to get a climate to their liking—are on the small side. More data, even of varying quality, tends to lead to better educational outcomes.

But amid all this contextual knowledge of students, there are also source of information that can be startlingly direct, even personal. The most obvious form is student writing. For the most part, grading student essays is an unpleasant task, in large part because students say predictable things badly. But every once in a while I'll be surprised by a revelation of a student's thinking that's arresting for its candor, insight, or both. More often than not, such writing has any number of problems on a grammatical or structural level. But even bad writers can convey a disposition or an ideology, whether they intend to reveal it or not. So it is that I occasionally learn just how narcissistic, narrow-minded, empathic, or insightful a kid can be. Sometimes I finish reading an essay just liking a student so much, marveling at an inexplicably attained preternatural wisdom, and thinking how marvelous it would be to be that person's friend. I'm reminded of that line from that adolescent perennial, J. D. Salinger's *Catcher in the Rye*: "What really knocks me out is a book that, when you're all done reading it, you wish the author that wrote it was a terrific friend of yours and you could call him up on the phone whenever you felt like it."[1]

But of course I can't be such a student's friend — not in that way, at least. I will on occasion seek out information about a student, using the school directory to determine a kid's address, parental situation, siblings, and the like. I may also strike up a conversation with a kid about weekend plans, the meaning of a slogan on a T-shirt, or who the student's other teachers are, hoping something interesting will shake out. Under certain circumstances, like walking together on a field trip, I might go further and ask the kid about what the parents do for a living, what schools she or he attended previously, and other biographical details. Occasionally a student will turn the tables and ask me such questions, which I'll answer reluctantly even as my esteem for the kid goes up a notch.

Every once in a while I'll find myself in among a klatch of students and manage to fade into the woodwork as they talk among themselves. It's in moments like these that I get a better sense of their standing with each other. There may come a moment when I'm drawn into the conversation — I'll agree that this musician really is awful or that movie was quite good — and for the briefest moment our respective social positions will vanish. For me such moments are tenuous; they tended to be tenuous when I was an adolescent, too. But I've never tried very hard to do much better in this regard. The truth is that I don't really want to be all that close to these kids. Most of the time I can't listen to them for more than fifteen minutes or so without getting restless. Part of this is envy — I don't want to press my nose against the glass — and part of is the knowledge that I have happily left some of the work they're doing behind.

Some of my colleagues finesse these interactions more effortlessly than I do. They seem to be able to tease, scold, cajole, even touch students and have it seem natural, and they can self-disclose with unselfconscious ease. And they do all this without compromising their integrity or authority. Such people, who are almost always a minority in a school, are indispensable. They're not necessarily good teachers in the conventional classroom sense of the term. But they're excellent educators and can make a deeper, more lasting impression than the most dedicated or brilliant instructor.

The final, essential point to be made here is that the information between student and teacher flows in two directions. All the ways I've been describing in which a teacher comes to know a student — facial recognition, initial impressions, community reputation, written communication, observed and direct conversation — also apply to the way a student comes to know a teacher. Indeed, many teachers are "known" to a student long before they have any idea who that student is. Individual student opinions can be idiosyncratic, conflicting, and poorly articulated. But the composite picture is usually reasonably accurate — or, at any rate, often no less so than the reputation a teacher has among peers.

Sometimes a student will teach you things about yourself. This might happen when you jump to a conclusion and a kid calls you on it, when you get a backhanded compliment that pains you in ways that weren't intended, or when you realize that your issues with a particular kid have uncomfortable affinities with your feelings about other kids in a specific demographic. Addressing such problems is not always easy, and actually correcting them may be impossible. But such feedback can be helpful in checking your impulses and sidestepping at least some mistakes.

Every once in a while you get a gift. Some years back I barked at a student who I felt was dragging her heels on doing her homework. This student didn't seem particularly engaged by my class, though I recognized an underlying intelligence and I knew that faculty and students regarded her highly as a singer and visual artist. But at that moment I was just annoyed. Later I learned that the immediate reason for my ire involved a misunderstanding. But even before that, I knew I'd been unfair—I'd just been diagnosed as diabetic, and I'd taken my distraction and irritability out on her. So I sent her an e-mail to apologize and explain my outburst. "I knew something was wrong," she told me the next day when I ran into her in an empty hallway. "That just wasn't like you." I found her compassion unexpected and moving, and it led me to disclose that my fear of aging had gotten the best of me. When I visited the college she went on to attend, I made a point of contacting her, and we had a lovely brief chat. I'm not sure I'll ever see her again (except on Facebook—I do a mass friending of graduating seniors each June, and she surfaces from time to time). But I'll always feel a tie to her.

Indeed, a great dividend of teaching is your former students. Sometimes—especially in the short term—relations with them can be awkward, because they come back from college all breathless and eager to speak with you, and you're still deeply immersed in a world they've left behind (a reality that I imagine is likely to inspire alternating relief and melancholy). But as they ripen into adults, you can lower your guard a little and converse with them in a manner that approaches that of peers. In a very few cases, you might actually achieve that point. Sometimes their affection for you is unstinting even as they surely see, perhaps with newfound clarity, the contours of your limits. They understand amid their own creeping mortality that it's important to honor vitality, however partial, wherever they find it, even if only in memory.

In the end, the most important curriculum a teacher will ever study is the student body. In time, the appeal of any given course will fade. But as long as you find the students interesting — as long as they entertain, bemuse, provoke, or enlighten — you'll have something worthwhile to do.

🐾🐾

"Mr. Dewey!"

"Natasha!" We embrace at the top of the stairs near my office. "How are you? How is Wesleyan?"

"Great! You look great!"

"So do you." She's lying; I'm not. A woman, not a girl. Short hair is better. She's learned how to dress, a sure sense of color. The winter coat she's got on is smashing. The scarf adds a splash of red. "What are you now, a junior?"

"A senior. Can you believe it?"

This is tricky. I don't want to start asking lots of questions about the thing I'm most curious about — her plans — because they're probably a source of anxiety. "No, but that's how these things go, Natasha. By the way, call me Horace."

A pained look crosses her face. "How is your sister?" I ask. "And Eddie?"

She brightens again. "Great! Catherine graduated from Amherst two years ago and is applying to law school for next fall. Eddie is working for Goldman Sachs."

"I'm not surprised."

"Well you know Eddie," she says. "What was it you said about Lincoln — 'his ambition was an engine that knew no rest'?"

"Good memory. That was Lincoln's law partner. And you turned out to be a history major — I remember from your last visit a couple years ago."

"And I turned out to be a history major," she repeats wistfully. "I'm thinking about graduate school."

"In history? God forbid, kiddo. You've got better things to do."

"Do I?" A retort laced with self-doubt. "I had a second major in East Asian studies. I went to China last year. I'm looking into doctoral programs."

Time to backtrack. "Well if anybody could get a professorship in this market, it would be you." I mean it. She was a wonderful student.

"I'm also thinking public history or material culture. I've got something lined up for this summer at the Met."

"Good for you."

"It's your fault, you know," she says, breaking into a smile and shaking a gloved finger at me. "Tenth grade. You got me hooked. And it was that paper on the Boxer Rebellion that got me interested in Chinese history."

I see her mother in the gesture. Lovely woman. I remember that my colleague Rick Engels once called her phony. I knew what he meant — she was always on, every time I saw her — but over time I came to see it as a matter of discipline. And generosity. Rich people can afford to be nice. That's why it's always a little surprising when they unreservedly are.

"And how about you?" she asks. "How are things going here?"

"Oh, you know. Same old stuff."

"What are you teaching?"

I tell her.

"You had a son who graduated too, right? Where is he?"

"University of Chicago. He's a couple years behind you."

"Wow! That's wonderful!" It occurs to me that this could sound condescending. But she makes it sound like my boy is now a starting quarterback for the Chicago Bears. Impossible not to like her.

The inevitable awkward pause has arrived. "Anyway," she says, gliding her sleeve back with one hand so she can see check her watch on the other, "I've got to run. But I just wanted to come by and say hello."

"I'm glad you did. Say hi to your family. And be sure to come by again after you graduate."

"I will," she says, as we hug again. "Great to see you, Mr. Dewey—I mean Horace."

"Likewise, Natasha. Take care."

It's only after I cease to hear the click of her boots on the stairs that I remember that her name isn't Natasha.

JEALOUSY

❧❧

"Caroline is absent?"

Advisory, a Monday morning in early October. It takes place after the first period of the day, when teachers take inventory of who's in school and who isn't. Advisory is also a clearing-house for information — announcements to make, messages to pass along, and the like. In that regard it essentially corresponds to what is sometimes called homeroom. But as its name suggests, advisory also carries with it connotations of advocacy and advice. You're supposed to be somebody a kid can turn to. You're also supposed to be a mediating figure between the student and the school, between the parent and the school (during twice-annual conferences), and, occasionally, between parent and child.

"I saw her in English," Annie Pence says.

Advisory is a bit of an institutional odd duck. Strictly speaking, an academic class is understood to be a random collection of individuals — teachers don't pick their students, and students don't pick each other. But with advisory there's a certain element of choice; kids often band together to form one in ninth grade, and teachers can choose which grade they will advise. There's an informal understanding that an advisory will stick together until graduation, though there's usually some moving around in the early years. I acquired the core of this group of seniors back when they were sopho-mores — others straggled in later, giving the group a polyglot quality—when my previous advisory graduated: a teacher unexpectedly left for another job after these kids finished ninth grade, so I stepped in, and have been with them for over two years now.

"Oooh," Robbie Menzies says. "Caroline is cutting advisory."

I've had a bunch of advisories over the course of the last fifteen years and would put this one somewhere in the middle. My first was a bunch of eight supercharged girls I inherited at the start of my East Hudson career when the colleague who forged them into a cohesive unit went on maternity leave. I brought them the cookies my wife baked once a week; they brought me the doting affection of adoptive daughters — a cake for my birthday; a Brooks Brothers tie at Christmas; a framed photograph at graduation that I still have on my desk. (Last week I had lunch with one of them; she's now finishing on a doctorate in comparative literature at Yale.) Then there was the advisory that graduated seven years ago, which included the advisee who had to be dragged across the finish line (he got an empty diploma case at graduation, with three weeks' worth of physical education to make up), the alcoholic movie-star mother who routinely mortified her daughter, and the divorced dad without custody who skulked during family conference night, collaring me at the end of the evening and pumping me for information about the son he hadn't seen in months. There's no drama with my current crowd. They did get some very nice "Dewey Advisory" T-shirts that they wear on special occasions. But there's not all that much of a spark either. We'll see if I invite them for a barbecue at my house come next spring.

"Looks like Caroline's headed for detention again," says Zack Thompson (he has a twin sister who's also a senior). We all get Robbie and Zack's irony: There's not much point in cutting a nonclass, and Caroline is about the last person you'd figure to cut a class in any case. The rest of the advisory is watching a Taylor Swift video on the Smart Board — "Could you turn that down?" I ask, and they comply — or doing their homework.

"How was your weekend, Mr. D?" Annie asks.

"Fine, thanks." Annie's a sweetheart and a fellow movie maven with whom I often discuss the latest releases. But I don't take the conversational opening today. I want to get attendance done and get back to the stack of papers waiting for me at my desk. "Since you saw her in English, Annie, I guess I'm not going to mark Caroline as absent."

"Caroline? Absent? How can you tell?" This from Danny Bell, who looks up from his Spanish homework.

"Stop it, Danny," Annie says. She's also the closest thing Caroline has to a buddy in the advisory. I don't know the backstory of how Caroline ended up in this group, which I find myself wondering about for the first time as I press the "apply" button on the smartphone app that allows me to transmit the day's attendance to the main office.

I also find myself remembering a lunchtime encounter a few days earlier with Jesper Nykvist, my longtime and much beloved colleague from the English department who has recently announced his retirement. Jesper teaches a section of the advanced senior seminar. A North Dakota native, he comes to work every day looking like a well-groomed farmer: flannel shirt, khakis, well-worn work boots. Insofar as there was ever any affectation in this — his father was the long-time pastor of a large Lutheran congregation — it's long since faded away. A quietly genial man who's handsome in a weathered way, Jesper conducts his classes from a Harkness table he built himself many years ago. When he does speak, it's usually to ask a follow-up question on a student's remark. He's one of those teachers whose classes are considered an experience; I've heard more than one kid say, "You can't leave East Hudson without taking Nykvist." My son tells me that the highlight of his high school career came during a discussion when he made a point about a Turgenev short story and Jesper said, "Huh. I never thought of that."

"Caroline Swanson," I remember him saying as he looked up from a spartan lunch of soup, bread, and water. "She's yours, yes?"

"She's my advisee. I've never taught her."

"Bit of an odd duck, if you ask me."

"Yeah?"

"Bright kid, no doubt about that. But she's mute in class. Which isn't a problem — there are plenty of kids who like to fly under the radar. But there's something strangely" — he shakes his head, looking for the right word — "*arrogant* about her silence. Like she won't deign to weigh in on the conversation."

"Huh. How are her essays?"

"Fine. She's a strong writer." (This is high praise; Jesper wraps his high standards in an understated manner.) "But I sometimes wonder if she isn't phoning it in. What do you know about her?"

"Not all that much. Mom's a psychiatrist; dad runs a landscaping company. They live in Yonkers. Caroline is a straight-A student, taking BC calculus. I think she's also a serious dancer, but that's out of school. A bit of a loner."

Jesper nods. "Makes sense, I guess. I can't say she's doing anything wrong, exactly. But she rubs me the wrong way." I'm surprised to hear Jesper saying this; if he ever criticizes students, it's usually in a mode of understated irony, something like "Well, Jonathan was never one to let a Dickens essay stand in the way of a good time."

Annie breaks my reverie. "See you tomorrow," she says as

she heads out the open door. "Thanks, Mr. Dewey," Robbie says out of habit as he departs. I remain at my desk, waiting for the rest of the advisory to file out. I've stood up to leave when Caroline sticks her head in — it appears she's been lingering outside. "Mr. Dewey? Can we talk for a minute?"

I'm surprised on multiple levels. First is the mere thought of Caroline skulking; she's always seemed so self-possessed. Second is the thought that she wants to talk to *me*. Our relations have never been anything but polite, at times even edging toward cordial (I remember being secretly pleased one day when she smiled at a dry comment I made about Mitt Romney). But I never had an idea that she regarded me as confidant material. My third source of surprise is that Caroline looks terrible. She's actually quite beautiful — aquiline nose, high cheekbones, lustrous black hair framing a face that I've mentally compared more than once to Katharine Hepburn's — though her severity of expression undercuts the effect: she's more intimidating than alluring (like Hepburn, I guess). But today her eyes look sunken, her demeanor agitated.

"Of course, Caroline. C'mon in."

Caroline enters. Then she does something that makes me deeply uneasy: she picks up the doorstop so that the door will close, leaving the two of us alone in the room. I feel an instant itch to walk over and open it again for my own protection. But I quell it — doing so would send a terrible message at a sensitive moment. *Focus, Horace. The kid needs you.*

And then Caroline does the most surprising thing of all: she breaks into uncontrolled sobbing. *Uh-oh. Does this mean I should hug her? Will that make her even more uncomfortable than it does me?*

"My gosh, Caroline! What's wrong?"

She shakes her head — I can't tell if it's because she's trying to say "nothing" or because what's distressing to her is too terrible to say. But her anguish overpowers my reservations, and I put my arms around her. I'm startled by how small, even fragile, she seems. Caroline's hands remain in front of her, but she puts her head on my shoulder. After a moment she pulls back. I yank a chair from a nearby desk and beckon her to sit down. I grab another and sit across from her.

She's composing herself. "It's Mr. Nykvist," she says.

My God. No. Not Jesper. My solar plexus contracts.

"I just got back my *Dubliners* paper.

Phew. I'm almost overwhelmed by a surge of relief. "Your *Dubliners* paper?"

"Yes. He hated it. He called my argument 'glib.' He *hates* me."

"No, Caroline. Absolutely not. Mr. Nykvist does not hate you."

"I worked *so hard* on that paper. And I *loved* that book. I just can't understand how he could call my thesis glib."

"Maybe you could talk with him about it?"

"I tried! I was just in his office! He said I didn't go deeply enough."

"Did you ask him if you could revise it?"

"He said no! 'Sometimes you've got to accept that you've simply come up short and move on,' he said."

This sounds surprisingly petty; I suspect there's a piece of this story that's missing. "Do you want me to talk with him?"

"It's no use," she says, shaking her head in despair. "I can't understand why he doesn't like me. Mr. Ramos was the same way. And Dr. Fisk. What's *wrong* with me? Why do they think it's necessary to be so *mean*?"

"Jealousy."

I say this without thinking, and instantly regret it. My colleagues Tom Ramos and Chris Fisk aside, I feel like I'm

betraying Jesper here, especially since I have a hard time believing he really envies anyone. His self-possession is one of
the things that make him so admirable. And a little intimidating. Even to me.

Caroline is incredulous. *"Jealousy?"*

I feel like I can't turn back now — it's my opportunity to
address an issue that I'm not likely to have again. "Maybe.
I don't know. Caroline, I'm not sure you understand how
you're perceived by some people."

She turns a little dismissive, her face taking on its familiar
contours. "Oh yeah, I do. I have to deal with it all the time.
But Mr. Nykvist? I just don't see it."

"Well, I don't know. I — "

"I thought he was better than that. People seem to think it
all comes easy to me. That I don't have to work hard. I thought
Mr. Nykvist understood that."

We have a moment of silence. I'm not sure what to say,
but I'm thinking I should say something. "Years ago there
was a movie called *Broadcast News*. In it Holly Hunter plays
a hard-charging news producer who's incredibly good at her
job. But her intensity also really gets on people's nerves. At
one point one of her colleagues says to her sarcastically, 'It
must be nice to always believe you know better. To always
think you're the smartest person in the room.' And she says
sadly, 'No, it's awful.'"

Caroline smiles — a dazzling smile, one I've never seen before. My God, there's a boy (or, who knows, a girl) at Princeton
or Stanford whose heart is going to break over that smile.

"People get unnerved in the presence of talent," I continue. "It makes them feel like they're missing something. In
order to feel secure with themselves, they have to imagine
hidden flaws. 'Sure, he's a great success on the job. But he's
got a terrible family life.' Or 'Yes, he's incredibly generous in

this way. Must mean he's a real jerk in that one.' I think this is going to be a burden that you carry, Caroline."

She nods; she knows. I sense impatience. Quit while you're behind, Horace. "Really," I say, not sure what else to. "I'll be happy to talk with him and see if he'll allow you to rewrite the essay."

"No, that's all right." She stands up, so I do too. "Appreciate this, Mr. Dewey." She extends her arms out, this time inviting the embrace, conferring a favor by way of thanks.

When she steps back, I take her shoulders in my hands and look her in the face. "You're all right, kiddo."

One more smile, a little perfunctory, before she heads to the door. "I'll see you tomorrow," she says.

And I do. But by that point she's gone. Again. For good.

TRANSIT

I notice that the fall foliage has peaked when I step outside the main entrance of the school and partake of the festive air as the school day ends. A string of school buses at the curb blends into the yellows and greens of the trees across the street; students tread across the freshly raked grass, backpacks casually slung over their shoulders. A group of boys cackles to my right, one of them exaggeratedly mocking another—"No, please, let *me* do it!"—and they all laugh hysterically.

"Jenneeeeee!" one girl calls another as they rush to embrace. "I got an eighty-seven," she says.

"Ninety-one," her long-lost pal replies. "I can't believe how easy that was." I can see a Latin textbook sticking out of her bag.

I'm struck, even shocked, by just how gleefully liberated these kids seem. No matter what they may have to do later, this is a moment of freedom. There's nothing else they're supposed to be doing—except boarding buses that seem more like props than vehicles.

Further ahead, a couple of students actually do climb aboard, and I can see indistinct silhouettes through some of the windows. Beyond the last bus, an ice cream truck is doing brisk business. Esteban Montoya, the maintenance guy, whom I found thumbing through a textbook in my classroom last week, is directing traffic, which has slowed to a crawl; a gust of wind swirls leaves around an SUV whose driver raises her hands over the steering wheel in frustration.

Belatedly, I see some familiar faces. There's Lisa Belkin

walking with Tom Edgerton, whom I taught last year. I didn't know they knew each other. Over there are Joey Gandolf and Nate Green; I remember Nate telling me that he and Joey live across the street from each other on either side of Broadway. Ginger Diamond, who is crashing and burning in my class, affectionately pinches the cheek of Peter Jacobs, a student who recently came out at a gay rights assembly. Sam Simkin is awkwardly lugging a guitar case onto the bus. Just as he does, members of the boys cross-country team jog across the street on their way to the park. Some of them will be catching the late bus at 6:15, when it will be dark. Right now the sun, which has been intermittent all day, is blanketed by cloud cover. It will not surprise me if a damp rain begins to fall any second.

A year from now, a decade from now, a lifetime from now, fragments of this moment will suddenly emerge, seemingly from nowhere: the cold gunmetal gray of a bus handrail; the smell of diesel fuel; "No, please, let *me* do it!" This will be what high school was about. Quadratic equations, haiku, and Alexander Hamilton will be the faded wallpaper. Lisa Belkin, Tom Edgerton, Joey Gandolf, Nate Green: they're here, in the eternal now.

Glad to have you with us.

GRADIENTS

I'm not surprised to see tenth-grader Olivia Gomez peering tentatively into my office on a Tuesday morning at 8:10, twenty minutes before the first class of the day. I've been enjoying a rare moment of leisure to thumb through the newly published student newspaper. (How much longer are they going to keep printing it? The school recently stopped distributing hard copies of calendars and directories.) Though Olivia's appearance is unscheduled, I received an e-mail from her father last night, a few hours after I returned an exam in which she scored a disappointing 69 percent, on the heels of 73 percent last time. "I'd like Olivia to come see you, so that we can understand what the problem is," her dad, Frank, had written. "We'd like you to explain how she can bring her grades up."

I might be wrong, but I sense Frank implying that Olivia's performance is my fault. But just as there are always a couple of kids like Olivia, who don't do well, there are others like Will Benson, who routinely aces exams from the start. Or Anna Gumm, who, after failing the last test, scored 87 percent on this one (I gave her a high five on her way out the door yesterday).

"Hi Mr. Dewey," Olivia says, courtesy mixed with listlessness. "Would it be OK if we talked for a minute about the test?"

"Sure, Olivia." I put the paper aside and swivel toward her. "Here, pull up a chair and have a seat."

Olivia sits down, glides out of a light jacket, and puts her immaculate backpack at her feet, rifling through it to pull out her exam, which she hands to me along with a stapled collection of pages that constitute her notes. They're densely annotated, with multiple colors of fluorescent underlining. Olivia puts her hands, face down, in her lap, and looks up. "Here's the thing: I studied so *hard* for that test. Like ten hours. You can ask my parents. They drilled me over dinner all week. It's just . . ." Olivia looks away and then returns to meet my gaze. "When I get in there I suddenly freeze up. I hope you believe me. I *know* this stuff. It's just when I see 'all of the above,' or 'none of the above,' or 'A & C,' I just lose all my confidence. My dad says . . ."

I look at the exam. I see a couple of cases where she had the right answer, erased it, and chose something else instead. When I look back at Olivia, her expression is positively grief-stricken. Sweetheart, I want to say, this just isn't worth getting that upset about. There will be other times for which that look will be all too justified. But not now, not yet.

"Let's get a few things straight, Olivia," I say. "First, I know that you studied for this test. I could tell from the way you were talking in our review session earlier this week. Second, I know that you know this stuff." In fact, I don't really know she does know it—she's memorized some information, for sure, but probably doesn't really understand it. But this isn't the moment to say that. "Actually if I had to guess, you probably studied too much, not too little."

I turn away from Olivia momentarily, hit a few keys on my laptop, and run my finger across an electronic ledger. "Look, Olivia, while your performance on the exam was not good, you're not in academic danger here. Taking tests is clearly not your thing. Other things are. I see here you got a B+ on the first essay, and I have you down for an A in class participation. So you didn't do well this time. Maybe you'll do better next time."

"I don't do well on *anybody's* tests."

"Well, that's no crime. In any case, I would never make that the only determinant of your grade. I would never even make it the *primary* determinant of your grade. It's just one thing. Other kids find tests come to them relatively easy. Or are just too shy to say much in class. That's OK, too. The important thing is to have a variety of assessments so that I can see who's good at what." (*And*, I think silently, *to see who's good at everything.*)

Olivia nods. But that's because she's trying to be agreeable, not because she feels much better.

"All this said, there's nothing that says you can't improve at test taking. You can. You absolutely can. And there are things we can do. The thing is, Olivia, you know the information but you have trouble *using* it. That might come with practice." Glancing at my bookcase, I have an idea. "You ever see those SAT II or AP History books?"

Olivia nods.

"Maybe you can pick up one of those and practice answering the questions from the period we're studying. You can get them at any bookstore. They also have a few old ones at the library."

Olivia nods again. Still no sale.

"Here's another thing," I say, flipping through the stapled collection of notes. This is a *lot* of material. Your goal should be to distill all this. Reduce it. I'm not sure how well *I* could memorize a stack of information like this."

"I try to write down what you say in class. It's hard to keep up with you."

"Then don't even try. Just sit back and take it all in. After all, I put my notes online. Maybe you can relate what you learned over dinner. Have a conversation about it instead of doing drills. Explain it to your parents. It's like what

Mr. Green"—my colleague in the religion department—"always says: 'If you can teach it, then you know it.'"

"I couldn't not take notes. I'd just be too afraid I was missing something important."

"Well, how about this: can you record our classes?"

"Record them?"

"Yeah, record 'em. You probably have an app on your phone. Or download a free one."

"Actually, I think I do have like a voice memo thing on it. My brother uses one on his phone to practice his singing."

"There you go. Why don't you give that a try?"

Olivia nods in agreement. She knows that's her job here. She's a better student than she knows. I would really like to get a cup of coffee before class.

"I don't know if any of these approaches will work," I tell her, trying to wrap up this encounter by conjuring up a plausibly hopeful script. "But they're worth a try. Maybe one of them will click and stick. I don't see how you have much to lose. The important thing to keep in mind, Olivia, is that you're really doing OK, whether or not one of these techniques turns out to be helpful. Keep up your class participation, do a bang-up job on the History Day project, and I'll bet you still end up somewhere solidly in the B range. But I do think that trying to meet the challenge you have with tests is worth trying to meet head on. How about you come see me before the next one and show me that study guide ahead of time? I may be able to help you winnow it a bit. Sound good?"

She smiles. "Sounds good to me." Ah, so *that's* what she wanted.

"All right, then."

Olivia stands up. "Thanks, Mr. Dewey."

"Hey, no problem, Olivia. Keep your head up. And be sure

to have a look at that excerpt from Seneca Falls Declaration of Sentiments tomorrow." She's probably read it already. But it will make her feel more confident if I remind her to do something that will come easily and naturally.

"I will," she says, getting up. "Thanks again." I wait a beat, flip the lid of my laptop closed, and grab the books I'll need for class. I'd rather walk alone right now.

It wasn't a great test, I think as I make a pit stop at the men's room on my way to the faculty lounge. The average grade was 82 percent, but I tossed two questions because they violated my "three-quarter rule" —whenever 75 percent of the students in a class get a question wrong, I conclude that there was a communication problem on my end, and everyone gets credit (students who answer it correctly get extra points). Sometimes I feel guilty about giving tests at all — compared to essays, they're irresistibly easy to grade, especially since I only tweak them from year to year, scrambling the multiple-choice items and substituting new short-answer questions. But I tell myself it helps get them ready for all those standardized tests, and it's a source of what I think of as quick and dirty information for report cards, inquiring colleagues and administrators, and students themselves. We're all addicted to numbers. Even when, as in the case of Olivia, they make us feel a little sick.

⁂

Actually, there are few forces more powerful in modern life in general than our collective longing for data. We want figures — to document our experience, to ratify our choices, or to help us make them. Perhaps because we're deeply aware of (and often inclined to celebrate) subjective experience, it becomes all the more important to establish metrics that offer the promise of pragmatic objectivity.

Sometimes such metrics are available — in doctor's offices, financial statements, or box scores. Yet even then ambiguities abound. Are the figures accurate? Which ones matter? Do they tell us what we want to know? Ironically, an abundance of data can sometimes multiply our sense of uncertainty: the unknowns are infinite. For some, this is actually a source of joy; economists and sports fans caress statistics with the same nuance with which litterateurs speak of fictional characters.

The quantitative imperative is as present in schools as it is anywhere else in American society. Budgets — for everything from buses to instruction — must be estimated. Time in the day must be subdivided. Credit, in the broadest sense of that term, must be extended or withdrawn. But there's one calculation in particular that looms larger than any other: the answer to the question "How am I doing?" The most intense, and controversial, metrics are those that measure performance.

In recent decades there's been a push by some politicians, educational reformers, and administrators to quantify the capabilities of students — and, indirectly, faculty — through standardized tests. Though opinions on the matter aren't entirely uniform, teachers are generally viewed as skeptical of this approach. This is widely perceived (by nonteachers, at least) as a matter of self-interest. Teachers don't want to be saddled with responsibility for student shortcomings on standardized tests, and they loathe the notion that their own performance can be reduced to a set of statistics. In the past they might have noted that the status of other professionals is not simply a matter of numbers, but these days doctors and lawyers are also increasingly rated by impersonal means (often, and always eventually, ones involving dollar signs). Most teachers don't reject the idea of accountability in the abstract. They will usually say that it should involve a series of factors, typically ones that give them plenty of wiggle room.

This hostility to quantification does not necessarily mean teachers are wrong. While a surgeon's success rate is certainly a figure likely to be of interest to anyone facing an operation, a patient's assessment of a given doctor is likely to be highly personal and impossible to quantify. Indeed, we sometimes overlook the way that all kinds of judgments in our lives are made without recourse to objective measurements for the simple reason that they're not available. On the other hand, teachers whose students consistently fail standardized tests are subject to harsh judgments from multiple sources.

Teachers are rarely in control of the standards by which they will be judged, since the terms are typically set by a school district, sometimes in consultation with a union. Nor can teachers escape the imperative to measure the performance of their students. Standardized tests aside, they're expected to collect and report their own data on their charges. This is widely regarded as among the most visible and important work a teacher does.

Most teachers would gladly avoid giving students grades: it's hard work to compile them, they invite invidious comparisons, and they're as likely to distract as they are to motivate. Most of the pressure to provide grades is external — graduates need them to get into other schools; administrators need them to document the work of the institution; parents seek indicators of progress (or lack thereof); students themselves want to know where they stand relative to their peers. Teachers will often use grades as a means of forming a casual, even private perception of a kid ("she's a B student"), but actually performing the calculations is a task that they would gladly abjure.

Among the most basic of the multiple headaches associated with grading is the sheer dreariness of numbing repetition. The time it takes to grade an individual piece of work may range from a minute to an hour, but even a simple quiz score must typically be calculated dozens of times. Moreover, you can almost never polish off a set of assignments in a sitting, if for no other reason than that deadline scofflaws, sick kids, or special circumstances keep you from getting the work when you want it. (Nagging them and administering makeup work are two more headaches.)

Once a set of essays, exams, or projects are graded, a teacher will be the bearer of bad news to at least a few people — sometimes a kid knows it's coming, sometimes a kid doesn't, and sometimes you'll be blindsided by their unforeseen disappointment ("I was really hoping to do better than a A−"). You may feel genuine regret in delivering a grade that's likely to pain the recipient; other times you brace yourself for grade grubbing, anxiety, or alarming resignation. Often valuable class time will be chewed up in assuaging fears before an assessment, answering repetitive and misguided questions. And it often happens afterward, too.

But all this is part of what might be termed the back end of the grading process. The difficulties actually begin much earlier, when you are trying to decide how a student will be assessed. This is not always under a teacher's control, whether because a class is preparing for a standardized test of some kind or because there's a prescribed curriculum from which a class is working. Still, there will often be intermediate steps, benchmarks of a teacher's devising, that will be administered along the way. The question will then be how to gauge student work effectively. Actually, a series of considerations must be taken into account before you even get to that point, among them these:

- What *form* will the pending assessment take (essay, test, group work, or something else)?

- *When* will I do it? (At the end of the unit? Are there holidays or special events in the way?)
- How much *time* should I put aside for the assessment? (How many nights' homework? Do I need review sessions or library visits? Will the assessment be executed during class? *Can* it be?)
- What *criteria* will I use to grade it? (Which questions will be worth how many points? How much room will there be for interpretation? Partial credit? How explicit should I be about what I'm looking for?)
- How will this assessment be *weighed* relative to ones that precede and follow it? (Will I permit do-overs? Include bonus or makeup provisions?)

A teacher won't or can't always know or foresee the ambiguities or complications an assessment will pose. But if you're a good teacher you will be thinking multidimensionally, hoping to avoid glitches — or worse, assessments that don't really assess the things that you think matter. Much of the time I don't really know if an assessment was any good until I see what students actually produce.

This is the hardest part: the formulation of *quality* assessments.[1] For tests, this usually means moving beyond regurgitation or comprehension and asking students to *manipulate* information. For essays or lab reports, it means asking questions that are legitimately open ended, inviting students to analyze events and arrive at independent conclusions. (This usually requires getting *you* outside the rut of your own biases, political and otherwise, which has the benefit of keeping you intellectually limber.) For group work it means creating opportunities to collaborate without insisting on exactly how it be done while providing some kind of checklist for marking progress. In all these and other cases, there should be some explicit or implicit intermediate steps by which students may arrive at satisfactory answers — which is to say answers that are in some sense right, as well as ones that permit students to feel like they've accomplished something meaningful. The most satisfactory assessments of all are likely to be ones where students themselves are formulating the questions, though this can be a complicated matter to engineer no less than to execute.

Once you've come up with a good assessment, you have to wage a little bit of a power struggle with your students in order to launch it. That's because their interests in the matter are not quite the same as yours. Of course you want them to learn, and of course they want to learn. But they often view this in terms of getting a good grade — "What do we need to know?" — and the grade can matter more than the learning. For them studying is a means to an end; for you the end is that *they will have studied*, that they absorbed material by reviewing or writing about it. Given that they're going to forget most of what you tell them sooner rather than later, it's the habits of thought, the process of mastery, even fleeting mastery, that matter more than the given information at hand.

Another source of conflict is that while they all want to do well, you're expected to design assessments where there is some variation in performance. You want to recognize — discern as well as reward — excellence, and you want to identify students who are having difficulties, hopefully because you can provide some measure of remediation. Most of the time, assessments that everyone fails or everyone aces are not desirable — even if you don't mind them, there are likely to be other constituencies who do, including students themselves.

This dual role of judge and coach generates the biggest dilemma of the teaching profession. Since your goal is to help students improve, and since encouragement is often the instrument of self-fulfilling prophecies, you're likely to be biased in favor of higher rather than lower grades. But students also crave challenges; rewards that are too easily given can prove paradoxically discouraging, both because they reduce incentives and because they deprive excellent students (who probably have little opportunity to demonstrate excellence in other arenas of their lives) of the chance to shine. This is why it's important for teachers to provide some variety in the kinds of the assessments they offer and, within the limits of their time, multiple opportunities to excel.

It's also important to separate — and be clear that you're separating — students' performance from your regard for them as people. For a new teacher, it may be a little startling to learn how much students care about what an individual teacher thinks of them, both because they believe in a causal link between likability and grades, and because students (especially adolescents) tend to be emotionally insecure. If asked, most teachers will say that some of their favorite people happen to be mediocre students, because teachers, whatever investment they may have in their discipline, know there's more to life than excelling at math or English.

One of the bigger challenges I face as an educator is sustaining a healthy pedagogical relationship with consistently subpar students. No one likes having to struggle with something that other people can do easily, and one of the great prerogatives of adult life is being able to walk away from academic subjects one doesn't do well. Students don't have that luxury, and having to spend multiple hours each week on a task that you not only hate but also feel you don't do well is a source of all-too-adult disillusionment. Such situations call for teachers to summon real imagination, as well as compassion, even as they recognize the limits of what they can do for any child.

For most of recorded history, an empirically established relationship between academic performance and success in adult life, as measured in terms of things like income and occupational prestige, has been hard to come by. In recent decades, however, there's been a growing perception — and a growing body of evidence — that in fact academic performance does correlate with success in such terms. Certainly a college degree has more economic value than ever before, and a degree from elite institutions translates into even greater value, less because of educational quality than of social connections. But here as in so much else, *success* is a complicated term with multiple metrics, and with values that lack any meaningful metrics at all. (How does one weigh, much less compare, creativity?) We may long for quantification, but, as I often say, life is an existential condition marked by insufficient information. The most learned people are those who are good at making educated guesses.

❦

Olivia pays me a visit before the next test, and we go over her review sheets, which are pretty good. (In all honesty, I don't know what her problem is.) When she scores 81 percent, I write "Progress!" across the top of her copy of the test. Her subsequent scores: 79, 84, 83, 80. Her midterm grade is a B; at the end of the year I give her a B+. This is padded; I put a thumb on the scale with her essays and class participation, because I fear that giving her anything lower will break her spirit. I worry a little that she'll become embittered if she ends up getting denied from the college of her choice because her standardized test scores and essay are decisively weaker than her grades, or if she gets into a demanding program only to find she's over her head. But I don't linger over such scenarios; they're too hard to predict, and if they do actually play out I'm not going to be around to witness them. Such is the blend of kindness and brutality that guides us as we plot our gradients.

One cool late afternoon in May, I notice that the girls' softball team is playing a home game, and I take a detour from the parking lot to have a look. The crowd watching the game is more sizable than I would have figured, perhaps because we're playing our crosstown rival. On the mound is none other than Olivia Gomez, whose visage has a fierceness I've never seen on her in the classroom. There are runners on second and third; I'm told our team is up by two runs and it's the top of the sixth. "Go Liv!" the spectators cheer. "Two more, two more!" Her next pitch blazes results in a swing and a miss: strike three. "Yes! Yes! That's the way you do it!"

Olivia's cheerleader in chief is Arianna Bergson, a senior shortstop who I'm told has been recruited to play for Amherst. "One more, Liv! One more!" The next pitch results in a ground ball that Arianna fields and throws to a first baseman I don't know. The crowd claps as Olivia's teammates converge to shower her with praise and affection. Just as she crosses the first base line, we make eye contact. I can't tell if she sees my thumbs-up. Or cares.

ROMANTICS

"OK kids, listen up!" Denise Richardson bellows to the crowd of students on the edge of Walden Pond in Concord, Massachusetts. "I'm going to go over the assignment one more time. You *must* follow the directions . . ."

I'm stunned by how beautiful the pond is on this autumnal morning. The foliage shimmers on the still water and bursts against the crystalline sky. Dubious about this part of the overnight field trip — instructing students to go into the woods and have a Transcendental moment strikes me as a contradiction in terms — I'm nevertheless delighted to be here. In the afternoon, I'll be one of a set of teachers leading classes along Boston's Freedom Trail. I'm looking forward to my annual cannoli at Faneuil Market.

I'm jostled back into attentiveness by an unexpected moment of silence that is apparently the result of Denise looking at her watch. "You will have fifty minutes," she tells the students. "That's enough time to walk around the whole perimeter if you want to, but you'll have to keep up a good pace." She turns and points to her left. "If you simply want to see the site where Thoreau had his cabin, walk straight this way. It will take you about ten minutes. Whatever you decide, you have to be back on the bus at 11:00 sharp. Hey! Alan!" Denise claps twice and points at a sleepy student I don't know (which is most of this batch). "To be awake is to be alive!" Some chuckle; I wonder if they get the allusion or are simply amused by the contrast between Denise's no-nonsense energy and Alan's torpor. "All right then," she concludes. "Go!"

The students stand around dumbly for a moment but

begin to disperse with growing momentum. "I'm going over to the gift shop," Denise tells me. "I have to make some phone calls. I'll be over in a little while to help round up this herd of cats." I nod and begin walking around the pond, beginning at the far side from the cabin site.

I have ambivalent feelings about Thoreau. I've no patience for the cranky misfit of "Civil Disobedience," who thought he could simply opt out of paying taxes he didn't like. And no man who has his mother and sister do his laundry can call himself self-reliant. But for all his prickliness, I sense an inner struggle to live the words, and I know that dismissing him as a phony is a little like complaining that sinning churchgoers are hypocrites: it's missing the point. I'm intrigued that Walden Pond is not, was not, the wilderness, but in fact is in easy walking distance from Concord village. I read that a railroad ran near the actual site of the celebrated cabin in Thoreau's time, and apparently still does. Looking ahead, I see a cluster of students and, off to the left, evidence of a railroad bed. I veer away from it so I can continue to savor my solitude.

I've rounded about two-thirds of the pond when I see two still figures lying side by side in a bed of pine about one hundred feet away. They are not engaged in an overt sexual act, but the sense of intimacy is unmistakable. From the angle of my approach I can see only sneaker bottoms clearly; the rest is partially hidden in evergreen. One kid apparently has his hands behind his head; the other appears nestled beside him. I don't recognize either, but either or both could be my students. Though I feel obligated to break up this idyll, I'm charmed by it. Years from now, long after Denise Richardson's (uncompleted?) assignment is forgotten, *this* will be what these two remember from this trip. Surely even a loner like Thoreau would, or should, approve.

I hear a voice shouting far to the right. "Horace? Is that you?" It's Denise, motioning a cluster of students to keep moving toward the group's starting point.

"Yes, Denise! It's me!" I respond forcefully. As I do, the two students scramble to their feet and begin running away, presumably to circle behind the cabin site and rejoin the group there. They both look like boys.

"Will you backtrack a bit and round up any slackers?" Denise asks.

"Sure," I say, turning around and walking in the opposite direction. While I scrunch my eyes, trying to determine if I recognize either student, I'm approached by my favorite kid, Wilhelmina Sperry, notebook in hand, clearly running to make up lost time and ground.

"It's OK, Willie," I say reassuringly. "Is there anybody else back there?"

"No. I'm the last one," she says as she slows to a walk, clearly out of breath. "I wanted to take a few more minutes to make some notes about a spider web I found. I guess I lost track of time."

"Good for you." Willie and I are now walking toward the bus at exactly the same pace.

"I love it here," she says. "That was a good assignment. Now that I've actually *seen* the pond, I need to reread the parts of *Walden* we discussed in class."

"Sounds like a good idea."

A pause. And then: "Mr. Dewey, would you call Thoreau a romantic writer?"

"Well, not exactly. Not in what I think of in the classic sense of the term, like Wordsworth or Shelley, who were British writers a generation or so before Thoreau. But I'm sure a lot of people would."

"I just love him."

"You're a generous soul, Willie. But remember: it's a big world out there. There are lots of fish in the pond."

Willie turns her head toward me. "You're not talking about how they restock the pond with fish."

"No, Willie, I am not."

Willie is beaming. "Don't worry, Mr. Dewey. I'll keep my standards up."

"Atta girl, Willie. Any writer would be lucky to catch you. Any nonwriter, too."

QUESTIONING

Late November: *The Adventures of Huckleberry Finn*. A few years ago I teamed up with two colleagues in the English and religion departments to team-teach this humanities course built around the theme of freedom. The course is divided into six units, each of which juxtaposes freedom to another concept that exists in some tension with it. So, for example, we open the school year with freedom and tolerance, reading *The Scarlet Letter* and studying literal witch-hunts and metaphorical ones (McCarthyism, allegorized in *The Crucible*, and the AIDS crisis, as depicted in *Angels in America*; the two are linked by the character of Roy Cohn, who plays a role in both). In October we have our next unit, on freedom and independence, in which we look at the American Revolution and Transcendentalist classics, among them Ralph Waldo Emerson's "Self-Reliance" and Henry David Thoreau's *Walden*. *Huck Finn* is a pivot to the next unit, on the relationship between freedom and slavery. The literary lineup there consists of poems by Phillis Wheatley, Frederick Douglass's slave narrative, and Toni Morrison's 2008 novel *A Mercy*, which looks at the earliest days of slavery. In every unit we juxtapose the literary and historical material to philosophy (e.g., Aristotle's notion of slavery) and modern-day analogies (is sweatshop labor a form of bondage?).

It was a real challenge to get this course off the ground, and it took a couple years of tinkering to get it right. But by this point we've got the curriculum down, notwithstanding the occasional substitution to keep it interesting — a Jhumpa Lahiri story on immigration here, a look at Native American steelworkers there. The canonical stuff like *Huck Finn* is perennial. As such, I find it a little boring. When you do the same book year after year, you tend to get lazy; I haven't actually reread the novel in years. I've got a well-annotated copy I review as we get under way for what ends up being about a two-week stretch of classes, and I'm probably one of the few people who use SparkNotes for its supposed purpose: as a means to review the book (as opposed to a substitute for reading it). Actually, my main source of preparation for class is the online forum in which students are required to post passages they find interesting and to explain why. I'll pluck out something I think has possibilities for close reading or note if there's a passage that gets multiple takers.

I've also got a few set pieces that I know from experience will generate a good conversation. One, of course, is the famous passage in chapter 31, in which anguished Huck, torn between returning lost property to its legal owner and helping that property — the escaped slave Jim, with whom Huck has been traveling — find his freedom, finally decides on the latter. "All right, then, I'll *go* to hell," he says, ripping up the note he'd written disclosing Jim's location.

My favorite discussion starter is more of a byway, one of many comic exchanges that pepper the novel. In chapter 23, Huck and Jim are saddled with the self-styled "Duke" and "Dauphin," a pair of rogues who fleece the denizens of Mississippi River towns any way they can, among them selling tickets for bogus Shakespeare performances and then skipping town before the victims can exact revenge. One night after a particularly good haul, Huck and Jim enjoy a rare moment of respite from the increasingly imperious demands of the sleeping hucksters and converse quietly on their raft. I have the passage from an online edition of the book on the Smart Board, which I read aloud:

"Don't it 'sprise you, de way dem kings carries on, Huck?"

"No," I says, "it don't."

"Why don't it, Huck?"

"Well, it don't, because it's in the breed. I reckon they're all alike."

"But, Huck, dese kings o' ourn is reglar rapscallions; dat's jist what dey is; dey's reglar rapscallions."

"Well, that's what I'm a-saying; all kinds is mostly rapscallions, as fur as I can make out."

"Is dat so?"

"You read about them once—you'll see."

Huck is speaking rhetorically here, I explain. Even if there was an obvious way to do so, Jim wouldn't read about them, because he can't: he's illiterate and he's a slave. Regardless of his location, learning to read would be discouraged if not illegal.

But Huck *is* literate. I remind students that we're told early in the book that he attended school regularly over a period of months, to the point where the tough-loving widow who's raising him says he was "coming along slow but sure, and doing very satisfactory." She's not even embarrassed by him anymore, he reports. Indeed, Huck's education might well have continued a good deal longer had not his ne'er-do-well pap returned. Irritated to learn that his son has been in school, Pap demands that he read a book. Huck obliges with "something about George Washington and the wars." Appalled, his father knocks the volume away. "If I catch you about that school I'll tan you good," he says. "First you know you'll get religion, too. I never see such a son."

To at least some extent, however, the damage has already been done. Huck summarizes the state of his education this way: he "could spell, and read, and write just a little, and could say the multiplication table up to six times seven is thirty-five, and I don't reckon I could ever get any further than if I was to live forever. I don't take no stock in mathematics, anyway."

But, I note to the class, he *does* take stock in history. There's an unmistakable overtone of pride as Huck explains to Jim why kings of all kinds are mostly rapscallions: "My, you ought to seen old Henry the Eight when he was in bloom. He *was* a blossom. He used to marry a new wife every day, and chop off her head next morning." Huck then proceeds to conflate the Arabian king of *One Thousand and One Nights* and Henry VIII with George III in a garbled account of the American Revolution (which we just finished studying, which allows the class to appreciate its absurdity):

> Well, Henry he takes a notion he wants to get up some trouble with this country. How does he go at it — give notice — give the country a show? No. All of a sudden he heaves all the tea in Boston Harbor overboard, and whacks out a declaration of independence, and dares them to come on. That was his style — he never give anybody a chance.

Jim listens attentively to this lecture. But he's tired of the royal scoundrels: "I doan' hanker for no mo' un um, Huck. Dese is all I kin stan.'"

Huck agrees. "But we've got them on our hands, and we got to remember what they are, and make allowances. Sometimes I wish we could hear of a country that's out of kings." Huck then goes to sleep, leaving Jim on watch as the raft courses the river. He later observes that Jim does not wake him when it's Huck's turn to cover.

I like this passage for a great many reasons, among them its transition to Huck's meditation on Jim's egalitarian decency: "I do believe he cared just as much for his people as white folks does for their'n . . . He was a mighty good nigger, Jim was." (And yes, I do use the N-word: to avoid it is to lose the painful, gorgeous irony in a great work of art. Students have trouble reading it aloud, as probably they should. But it's my job to say it plainly, without apology or indulgence, so not to fetishize a term that continues to be of unhealthily obsessive interest.) In any case, the principal pedagogic value of the whole rapscallions discourse is the way it serves as a springboard for discussion: What does Huck have wrong in his notion of history? What does he have right? How well do *you* know this history? How much do the facts matter in terms of Huck's larger point? What *is* that point? And so on.

So it is that when I walk into the classroom for what will be inaugural discussion of *Huck Finn* on a chilly but brilliant autumnal day, I'm a little rusty but ready to improvise. I've got to pocket this favorite passage of mine, because it will be a few days before we get there. So instead I'll ask the students to summarize the novel through the first eight chapters, which is a relatively easy point of entry as well as a device to jog my memory. "So gang," I ask, raising a steaming paper cup of coffee to my lips, "who is Huckleberry Finn?"

I sip in silence. Damn. This is a misfire: I intended a kid to say something like "He's a boy from Missouri who's running away from his father," and I'd take it from there. But it seems my query has been heard more interpretively and thus is difficult to answer, as if I were expecting something like "He's an empathic pragmatist in a morally corrupt social milieu." I put my cup down on my desk, wait a beat, and say, "He's a very *blank* person who *blanks*. Go ahead in fill in those blanks."

Still nothing. And then Alba Monteiro—decent student, though her last essay was all over the place—blurts out, "He's obsessed with death."

I think: *Blech.*

I say: "Interesting, Alba. Can you elaborate a bit?"

Kim Anders—puckish sense of humor, volleyball team, got an 89 on the last test, litigated another three points out of me—says, "Yes! I was thinking the same thing!"

What *wavelength* are these kids on?

"OK," I say. "But why?"

Kim continues her interruption of Alba. "Well, his mother is dead, right? That's like the first thing we're told."

"Well, yes, we're given to understand that. But where do you get the idea of this death fixation?" I know I sound little impatient, but I think it's a fair question, and I think in any case that I can get away with posing it, even with some irritation, to Kim.

But it's Alba who jumps back in. "It says right here on page 6 that the widow read to him about Moses. 'She let it out that Moses had been dead a considerable long time; so then I didn't care about him; because I don't take no stock in dead people.'"

"Hmmm. So the fact that he's talking about a dead person—says he doesn't *care* about dead people—is evidence of an obsession."

"Exactly."

Huh? I'm about to argue the point but stop myself. "What do the rest of you think? Do you agree with Alba and Kim that Huck has a death fixation?

I scan the faces in the room. Steven Gridley—skinny, unkempt, acne-riddled—is looking out the window. Tommy Giddens is whispering to Zak Finisteri. Cara Millberg is staring at her laptop. Evelyn WuWong is looking at me expectantly. She's paying attention but clearly has no intention of jumping into the fray. What's the term? Bright Eyes. But that's Japanese. Evelyn is Chinese.

Cara, who has permission to take notes with the laptop but in all likelihood has been shopping for shoes, looks up. "He's just so, what's the word—you know, when you're just only reacting to what other people do—"

"Passive?"

"Yeah, passive. Like he's so obsessed with what Tom Sawyer thinks."

"Yes, Cara, I think you make a very good point. But what does that have to do with being obsessed with death?"

"I dunno. It's just, like, he's not living. It's almost like he's a zombie."

There's something incongruous about Cara Millberg— the very embodiment of rude good health—talking about death. It seems so remote that she can barely talk about it coherently. And yet she's not entirely wrong. And, sure as she's sitting there, death, like that character in the Emily Dickinson poem, will be coming by to claim her. For the first time, I'm curious about what will happen to her in the meantime.

"I'm a little confused," I say, returning my gaze to Alba. "How can you be obsessed with death at the same moment you're saying you don't put no stock in dead people? Isn't that a contradiction?"

Alba narrows her eyes, taking the question in. Is she going to be able to parry it? If she doesn't maybe I can steer this conversation back on course—or, maybe more accurately, out of the gate. I'm thinking the opening of chapter 4, in which Huck talks about his schooling (he could "spell, and read, and write just a little, and say the multiplication table up to six times seven is thirty-five"). Can't go wrong talking about education with high school kids.

But now it's Alec Wearn—Dad writes for the *Times*; apparently he's a serious guitar player—who enters the fray. "What's with the staging his death thing?"

"Staging his death thing?"

"Yeah. When his dad starts beating him. He makes it look like he's been killed."

"Right. That's how he makes his escape. It's a means to an end. Doesn't mean he's obsessed with death, does it?"

"Kinda weird, if you ask me."

I guess I did ask. Maybe these kids are onto something. "I think Huck is depressed." This from Dana Weiss. Figures. It's not the first time I've heard therapy-speak from her. I remember her once referring to Arthur Dimmesdale of *The Scarlet Letter* as having low self-esteem. Tell me Mom *isn't* a psychotherapist.

"Depressed, huh?"

"Yeah. I think so. I actually read ahead a little bit to the whole Grangerfords and Shepherdsons clan war thing. That whole part about Emmeline Grangerford. After she dies Huck seems really upset. It's interesting after the whole Moses thing Alba just read. It's like this is the first time he allows himself to really grieve. And then he says something like 'I don't want to talk about it.'"

I'm a little stunned by this insight. My memory of the book is sketchy, but I know what Dana is talking about.

"Thanks a lot for giving the plot away!" Kim exclaims.

I'm about to try to explain to Kim that it's not that big a deal when suddenly the fire alarm goes off. Damn. I remember the assistant principal telling me yesterday we're behind on the quota that the state mandates. "Oh!" Dana says, genuinely upset. Steve Gridley looks like he's just received a get-out-of-jail card. As per our protocol, we file out of the room and out of the building silently.

As I shiver on the sidewalk, waiting for the all-clear, an essay question begins to take shape: "Some observers of *The Adventures of Huckleberry Finn* [wink, wink] say that the Huck

Finn we meet at the start of the story is suffering from depression. Do you agree? If not, why not? If so, explain why—and where, if anywhere, you think that begins to change. Be sure to use evidence from the novel to support your thesis." Gonna have to think about the depression thing—how to define it. Then again, let's see if any of them do it. I'm always talking about defining your terms. Maybe a few of them will.

"Two down, six to go," my colleague Eddie Vinateri says of the fire drills as we get the signal to head back into the building. After a pause, he gestures toward my clutch of returning students, a few of whom have, unaccountably, taken the book out with them. "How's humanities going?"

"Good," I say. "Class teaches itself."

GINGERLY REVISING

Ginger Diamond has come to see me to talk about her latest essay. This is a meeting neither one of us particularly wants to have — she surely dreads it; I'm knee-deep in the middle of recalibrating my spring semester syllabus when she arrives. But now that our unplanned encounter, largely orchestrated by others, is happening, we're both doing our best to make it worthwhile.

I've known for weeks now that Ginger is a weak student. Utterly silent in class, she never handed in her first essay of the new semester, and when I asked her about it a couple days after it was due, she said that she had a bad Internet connection. That's fine, I said, just give me a hard copy to-morrow. When that didn't happen, she said she was hav-ing printer problems and would drop it off later that day. When *that* didn't happen, I sent an e-mail to her parents. The essay materialized the next day, along with apologies for the delays from them and her. It was only minimally acceptable in terms of content and structure, but I decided that this was not a good time to tell her to do it again — I inferred I'd already caused some tumult in her household, and establish-ing a reputation as a remorseless academic stalker would not be the best way to promote a working relationship. But clearly I was going to have to keep an eye on her.

Her next essay, handed in on time, was even weaker. In my comments I beat around the bush a bit, commending her for her evident engagement and willingness to grapple with the question, but finally confessed that I found it — hesitating to use the word, but deciding it was best — "incoherent." I asked her to come and see me so that we could plot a course for revision. I felt both justified and guilty for this approach.

Justified, because I felt it important to be both willing to help and to ask her to take responsibility for her work, and guilty because I was asking her to demonstrate a level of maturity she'd already shown she lacked, and so nothing was likely to come of my overture, which would arguably leave me off the hook. I always feel a tug between trying to nudge my students along and protecting my time, and at some level I knew that if I wasn't more proactive with Ginger, she'd slip my mind. As indeed she did.

It was her parents who pushed the process along, sending around group e-mails to her teachers asking for feedback about her work a couple weeks later. A flurry of cc'ed exchanges with her adviser followed, which culminated in a phone call from the school learning specialist telling me that she happened to be with Ginger and wondered if she could send her my way. Yes, I said, turning back to my work with the added fervor of knowing it was going to be interrupted momentarily.

Now she's here at my desk, backpack at her feet, awaiting her fate, her sense of vulnerability so palpable that it overrides any other attribute. I try to set her at ease. Where do you live, Ginger (uptown), what do you your folks do (they're both on the business side of the television industry), do you have any siblings (an older half-sister from Dad's previous marriage). Her answers are direct, earnest, and dead ends. This is not a conversation.

"What do you do for fun, Ginger?"

"I dunno," she replies. "Nothing, really." Then, brightly, as if she's suddenly realized the solution to an algebra problem that's been posed to her: "I decided this week to work on sets for the spring musical!"

"That's great," I say, wishing I could make that ember flare. But I don't have the presence of mind to ask what she's making, how the show is going, or something to keep the momentum going. The only thought that comes to mind is that she'll have one more reason to put off grappling with her academic difficulties.

We proceed to talk about her coursework. Usually math and science are harder than history and English, but this year it seems to be the other way around. Last semester's history teacher was different, she tells me. More fact-based and smaller, more manageable, assignments. From another kid, this would be barely veiled criticism. I don't think she means it that way, though perhaps she should. But we need to get down to the business at hand.

"So what did you understand my message to you to be in my comments?" I ask. This is a standard gambit of mine; it's helpful for students to interpret what I said in their own words, and for me to be reminded, dozens of essays and often weeks later, about what I said to one kid in particular.

"That I was incoherent," she replies. Ugh. She got that message all right.

I prompt her to tell me what she was thinking about when she was writing the essay, and once she gets launched on a little soliloquy, things get easier. I jot down some notes as she talks, structuring her various points into a simple outline. The essay she's narrating is rudimentary and doesn't quite answer the question I ask. But if she can actually execute what she's saying on paper, we'll be making a definite step forward.

I show her the outline. "Does this make sense to you?"

She looks at it intently. "Yes," she says. "I had a pretty clear idea when I sat down, but I felt like I had so many ideas in my head, and I have attention deficit issues, and I dunno . . ." Her voice trails off.

So that's it: a learning disability. I really should have been thinking about that. I probably have a digest of her psychological evaluation, issued by East Hudson's Learning Center, somewhere on my computer. But there are so many now—something like a quarter of the student body has them, a number that keeps growing—that it's hard to keep track. In part, that's because any parent with a couple thousand dollars can get a psychiatrist to recommend special treatment, and when I look at such lists I see names of some kids I consider some of my best students who have taken out what seems to amount to an insurance policy for extra time on tests. I know I shouldn't think that way, especially since I have a child who's been diagnosed on the autistic spectrum, but I've become a bit cynical about it all. Ginger's certainly not gaming any system; indeed, she's dangerously close to falling through the cracks, and I'm part of the problem. And unlike that of a growing legion of students, the work I'm seeing is clearly her own. Praising the essays of overreaching private tutors has become something of a running joke among some of the faculty.

Ginger is interprets my silence as a prompt for further disclosure. "I don't like my meds," she says. "I hate the side effects." She looks away. This obviously hurts. But it's apparently what she's supposed to do, and she's going to play her part.

"I sort of understand," I tell her. "I have a kid with learning disabilities. I won't tell you I know what that's like, but I think I have some notion of the issues." She looks me in the eye for the first time. She understands my gesture for what it is, and her acknowledgment feels like one in its own right.

My problem now is that I don't know where to go with this. I know it's very easy to say the wrong thing—promise too much, offer too little. Our silence is awkward. Ginger pulls together the two sides of the unzipped hoodie she's wearing over her T-shirt, something she'll do repeatedly in the remainder of our meeting. This saddens me.

Back to the task at hand. She's going to work off the blueprint she has dictated to me. She asks when I want the revised version. I ask when's good for her. She tells me to tell her. How's Friday? All right, then. We agree to meet again before an upcoming test (she'll hand in her exam long before her allotted time is up and will score 71 percent, thanks my giving her the benefit of the doubt on some questions). "This is going to work out fine," I tell her. "I know it's hard — it's hard for everyone, no one writes effortlessly — but it's going to be fine." She smiles at me, hopefully and doubtfully, as she returns her papers to her backpack and zips it up. Our meeting is over.

Mom will follow up with an e-mail; I promise to read multiple drafts. But it's been a few weeks now, and nothing has happened. Ginger avoids eye contact again whenever possible. Maybe she'll pull things together on my watch, or someone else's. She has the good fortune — if at times she surely regards it as a mixed blessing — of people looking after her. But for me the whole encounter is a reminder of the limited ability of teachers generally, and this teacher in particular, to fill the unaccountable holes that riddle our lives.

NATIVE INTELLIGENCE

There are some topics in the survey that I regard as chronic problems in my teaching. I don't devote enough time to the Constitution. Latinos are stinted—they fall out of the picture once the focus shifts from Spanish colonization, to surface again only briefly during the Mexican War—and my handling of women's suffrage is weak. From time to time I resolve to fix these problems, but the press of other commitments often leads me to defer them. Sometimes, though, I do plug holes. This is the year I finally do something about Native Americans.

To some extent, I was spurred by an exceptionally talented former student who had spent a summer on a Lakota Sioux reservation and did a senior project, supervised by a colleague, to develop a curriculum for teachers of US history at the school to incorporate into their classes. So now that we've reached the late nineteenth century, and I've reached the point where I do my standard routine about the trans-Mississippi west, I add a session using her material on the massacre at Wounded Knee in 1890. I also toss in some material on the second Wounded Knee, the standoff at the Pine Ridge Reservation that took place in 1972. The latter event was marked by internecine conflict between tribal leader Dickie Wilson and his militant challenger Russell Means of the American Indian Movement (AIM).

After providing some overview information, I begin our class discussion by explaining how it is that they came to be assigned this material, and I recapitulate some of the history we've already studied. I also take what I consider a fairly standard gambit in asking them to compare the situation of Native Americans with that of African Americans. They're pretty quick to make the point that African Americans were pulled into the United States and absorbed, albeit unequally, into American society, whereas Native Americans, already here, were pushed out. They don't have the background to talk about the sense of militancy that the two groups shared after the integrationist spirit of the early civil rights movement; that will be a conversation for another day. For now, I ask: Do they think AIM was right to create that standoff? Was it the best strategy to get the US government to rethink its treaty obligations?

A long silence—a *very* long silence. Even when I paraphrase the question, I still get no takers. Did they do the reading? Did I make a big mistake by inserting this material into the course this way? In any case, we've fallen into a real ditch. I'm really not sure what to do.

Sam Stevens tentatively raises a hand, out of what I sense to be courtesy more than anything else. "I'm not sure taking over property and handing out guns is ever really a good idea," he says. A sensible answer from a sensible kid.

"But how else were they going to get the government's attention?" I ask.

"Well, civil disobedience," he says. "I mean, Martin Luther King used nonviolence, didn't he?"

Kim Anders steps in. "You know, I really don't know whether they had to do this or not. I just don't feel like I know enough to say."

Hmmm. If anyone did the reading, it was Kim. I'm about to ask what she feels she needs to know in order to have an opinion, when I suddenly change my mind.

"All right, then," I say, shifting my gaze from her to the class as a whole. "Let's approach this from a different angle.

Let's say you're a government official with responsibility for law and order in South Dakota. You hear that a group of militants have taken over buildings in a town, and it's your job to deal with the situation. What's the first thing you consider in deciding what to do?"

"Well, the first thing I'd want to do," Cara Millberg says, "is get over there and find out what's going on. Talk to them. Hear their side of the story."

Tommy Giddens makes a scornful face, which I sense is partly an exaggerated sense of playacting and partly reflects his actual stance. "What, Tommy, you don't think talking to the Indians is a good idea?"

"Oh, you know me," Tommy says. "I always shoot first and ask questions later." Zak Finisteri laughs silently; Tommy punches his upper arm.

"Seriously, though," I continue, "where would this go? First these people make a bunch of demands that people try to listen to, and then where does it end? Soon every Indian tribe is complaining and there's a casino on every corner." Real laughter at this. In our part of the world Indian policy isn't much of an issue on a local level, but we've made field trips to the Mashantucket Pequot Museum in Connecticut in previous years, and I've listened to kids on the bus express unease about whether it's really right for Native Americans to profit from gambling.

"Tommy's right," Kim says. "You gotta keep 'em in line."

"So there you have it," I say, trying to string these two opinions into a conversational clothesline. "Cara says hold discussions; Tommy takes a hard line. What say the rest of you?"

Alba Monteiro weighs in. "I think that one thing Tommy doesn't get is that we're talking about a group of people who have had a really bad time. They're people who have been oppressed for, like, centuries."

"Actually, Alba," I say, seizing on an opening here, "you're not so much disagreeing with Tommy—well, you are kind of doing that—as you are suggesting an entirely separate way of dealing with the problem. Cara's instinct is to go local. Tommy's instinct is to apply broad principle, in this case to combat what might be termed the problem of the slippery slope. There are, by the way, psychologists who would say that these are gendered ways of conceiving the situation—men tend to apply rules, while women tend to think in terms of relationships." Tommy gives Zak a fist bump. "But you, Alba, are a girl after my own heart, because your instinct is to think in terms of history."

"History?" Tommy asks. "What's history?"

"Actually," I say, ignoring him, "I think there's something important here that goes beyond Native American history. Kim said she felt like she lacked enough information to make an intelligent choice, and in an important sense she is of course right. But the truth of the matter is that this is really what life is like a lot of the time: you're forced to make decisions based on incomplete information. What car should I buy? Whom should I marry? Do I take that job? Should I invest in this company? If you knew everything there is to know, making a choice would be easy. But you almost never do. So what you're left with are instincts, what your gut tells you. But what's the *source* of your gut instinct? Is it facts on the ground, like Cara? Abstract principles, like Tommy? Or experience, like Alba's? Do you say, 'What features does this car have?' Or 'I like this company's products'? Or 'I have a lousy track record with blonds'?" Some smiles here. "Knowing how your gut works—and, maybe, making that gut bigger or changing its chemical composition—could give you better digestion, if you know what I mean."

"This is getting pretty gross," Kim says.

"Sorry. I guess I was getting a little carried away."

"You were also acting out of ignorance," Tommy says.

"Well, that was sort of my point," I reply.

"Yes, well, I think I need to enlighten you. Have a look at the clock. Class is over."

He's right. "Thank you, oh wise one."

"De nada," he says, closing his textbook. "Happy to help in your search for wisdom."

Damn. I thought I was pretty good. But I guess nothing trumps the clock.

(DANGEROUS) DIVERSITY

The story, which I distribute in hard copy as students enter the room so that they can refer to it later, and which I read to them after everyone arrives, goes like this:

PREP SCHOOL WEIGHS PROMOTING INCEST
Request from advocacy group attracts supporters, criticism

The elite East Hudson School, an institution catering to wealthy New Yorkers, may extend an invitation to the Cleopatra Society, an organization promoting sibling marriage, according to sources close to the school. Society president Phil Delphi confirmed this week that he has made the request of East Hudson Dean of Students Edie Widmer, who told him she would consider it. "We believe that whatever happens among consenting adults is their business," Delphi wrote Widmer in an email dated February 30, "and we wish to educate your students to combat the prejudices and legal restrictions that have too long surrounded our identity." Neither Widmer nor senior administrators would comment on the request. A Town Hall meeting to discuss the proposal is scheduled for this evening.

If honored, East Hudson, which calls itself a "progressive" institution, would be the first high school in the country that agreed to host the group. Delphi said 14 previous high schools had turned him down without discussion. The Cleopatra Society has made presentations at Reed and Oberlin Colleges as well as the University of Southern Maine.

East Hudson is no stranger to controversy. A 2011 assembly on Israeli-Palestinian relations drew sharp protests, was cancelled, and then followed up with another event that drew crowds on the street outside the school building. There are frequent complaints about Political Correctness among faculty and students.

A petition signed by 421 of the school's approximately 600 students affirmed their desire for the assembly. "We believe the Cleopatra Society should be allowed to speak," the document reads. "It's a free speech issue and a diversity issue. Not all of us believe in incest. But we believe that open discussion is the basis of a true education."

Others are not so sure. "I can't tell you how stupid this is," said French teacher Terry Franowicz, who's been teaching at the school for 31 years. "As if every crackpot idea deserves a crackpot hearing. Forget about free speech. Life is too short. So are my classes. We've got better things to do than allow an inane controversy to bring the school to a halt. That's why the kids signed the petition. To avoid homework."

Parent Leslie Gaynor's objection is rooted in the subject of the proposed assembly itself. "It's offensive," she said of the Cleopatra Society's request. "I'm a believer in progressive education, but incest isn't an issue. It's a crime. People have been hurt. There is a line, and we have to draw it. If everything is open to discussion, then nothing is off-limits."

Another parent, Tim Reed, disagreed. "The issue here isn't whether you think incest is right or wrong," he said. "It's whether students and educators can be trusted to discuss and think for themselves. That's what this place is supposed to be about."

"It's the last straw," said Red Moody, class of 1966. "I've been a faithful alumnus, but I barely recognize the place anymore." Moody said he has decided not to make the third six-figure gift to match ones he made in 1996 and 2006. "I've always thought of myself as a liberal, but this is just going too far. And I know for a fact that I'm not the only one who feels this way."

"Sounds like East Hudson, all right," said Jette Black, Class of 2015, who is now in her first year at Princeton. "College has been downright boring by comparison. The only thing we do for fun is drink.

After the news story is distributed, I hand out a set of index cards randomly. On each one is an identity: student, faculty, parent, alumnus, trustee, and others (along with a few wild cards). One student gets the card for Head of School: I ask that student to come to the front of the room. At the end of class, it will be that student's decision whether the assembly proceeds or not. I am the Head of School's executive assistant, and will preside over the town hall. When time runs out, I'll explain that the Head must leave for a very important but unspecified meeting. Until then, participants are to make their case in the town hall meeting as persuasively as they can. They can say whatever they want, but it must be from the perspective, as they interpret it, that's on their card.

As you might imagine, the quality of the conversation and its outcome vary widely when I run this simulation. Some kids are fast on their mental feet; others doggedly push their own perspective through the mouth of the role they're expected to play. This is easy for the ones playing students: most want the assembly to proceed. The parents tend to be divided. Some profess disgust; a few say it's important to keep an open mind. One of the roles I deal out is that of the school's director of development; it's not hard to steer this student to say that the controversy is hurting fundraising, and sometimes the kids playing alums will second that. Once, when I demonstrated this simulation with my colleagues, a faculty member argued against the assembly so eloquently that the teacher playing Head of School cited his testimony as the reason for her decision not to allow the assembly. Only then did he reveal his card: incest survivor. Other times are not as successful. The last time I ran the simulation, two students holding that card described incest in glowing terms: everyone should try it. Not what I had in mind.

Still, I reasoned, the risk of such outcomes is outweighed by the benefits. Chief among them is a genuine sense of unpredictability that gives students interest—and a stake—in the outcome. In addition to pro and con arguments on the merits of the case, there's usually one argument that emerges about whether this topic, however one feels about it, is really a relevant or appropriate focus for school time and attention.

These conversations can get quite spirited. I know I'm pushing the envelope with this one: incest is not usually considered an acceptable topic for public discussion among adolescents. But I feel pretty confident it's worth it.

Confident, that is, until I run the exercise with Evan in my class.

🍂🍂🍂

I knew about Evan years before he enrolled in my course: a kid in an electric wheelchair tends to stand out. I would give him a polite smile on those rare occasions when we actually made eye contact passing in the hallways. We don't have a lot of disabled students at my school; it's a veritable nightmare as far as handicapped accessibility goes. The administration has complied with the 1990 Americans with Disabilities Act by chipping away at the problem gradually, adding ramps every time renovations are made. Last year, at great expense, a nurse's office and some library space were commandeered for the construction of a new elevator, an installation that took most of the summer.

From what I gleaned at the faculty lunch table, Evan came to the school in ninth grade after being homeschooled by his mother. He has muscular dystrophy, a congenital neuromuscular disorder in which muscle (which includes his heart) gradually turns to fat. Life expectancy is somewhere in the twenties, though I'm told it's improving. Evan, my colleagues say, is a serious, successful student who appears to be well liked by his peers. As one of his teachers notes, he has a notably pleasant face, even as it's clear that his body, usually encased in jeans and a plaid shirt, has been distorted by the disease.

Accommodating Evan means that my class has to meet in a different room than it usually does, something that dismays me — and dismays me for dismaying me. But I make my peace with that relatively quickly, as I do his late, slightly disruptive entrances, the result of the circuitous route he must take in order to make it to class. But he's a model classroom citizen: quiet, attentive, and usually good for a few mild-mannered, thoughtful remarks in our class session. Whether it's a product of his experience or of our tendency to project wisdom onto him, Evan seems mature beyond his years. That said, I can't say I really know him. I hold the door for him and engage in chitchat about the weather, or how about those Jets, but haven't had a real conversation with him. Then again, I don't typically have real conversations with any of my students outside of class. I'd like to with Evan, but I'm just not sure about where or how to start.

On the day of our Cleopatra Society simulation, Evan draws a student card. The discussion that follows is generally unremarkable; he chooses not to say anything. Because he cannot raise his hand, I periodically look in his direction to see if he has anything to say. He doesn't, but he seems to give rapt attention to the proceedings.

As is my custom, I end the simulation a few minutes before the end of class to give students the chance to debrief. What do you feel you've learned? I ask the class.

"I thought it was really good," Charlotte Sampson, a terrific kid, says. "I never thought about these issues before."

"It's hard, because you have to think about the perspective that you're given," says Jake Agnelli, who vigorously protested the idea of the assembly as an alum. "You can't just say what you want."

"I think the gay marriage analogy really works," says Molly Edwards, who pressed the comparison between incestuous marriage and gay marriage as a student (we now allow one; why not the other?). I regard such comments as boilerplate stuff. Most of the time kids will say an exercise went well even if it didn't. To get anything useful out of them, you usually have to prod and be genuinely critical of yourself. I'm about to ask Molly *how* the gay marriage analogy works when I hear a query from the other side of the room: "I have a question."

This from Amir Zaman, a student with a serious mien. Long commute to school every day. Mom works for the post office; Dad's not in the picture. These are things I learned on a recent field trip when I struck up a conversation with him. I recently gave Amir an extra copy of the assigned book we were reading, not clear whether he actually lost his but getting the distinct impression that acquiring another one would be a significant financial challenge. "I wanted to ask this earlier," he's saying, "but I didn't get a chance to. Don't children who come from incest end up with serious problems? Like diseases?"

"Well, yes, possibly," I reply. "Hemophilia, a blood disease, is often cited because it affected the royal families of Europe about a century ago. But remember, people who marry don't necessarily have children. And there's screening and counseling now for any number of genetic" — I'm mindful of having to choose my words carefully with Evan in the room — "issues."

Unfortunately, Amir is not choosing his words carefully. "Well, I just think these people need to be careful so that they don't make a big mistake."

Ugh. I can see a look of concern register on the faces of a couple students quick enough the grasp the implications of what Amir is saying. I check an impulse to look at Evan — I sense it would be awkward — even as I'm aware in my peripheral vision that he would like to have my attention. But Charlotte has raised her hand, and even though I should probably be picking someone who hasn't spoken already. I point to her, hoping she can lead us to safety.

And she does, sort of. "I think it's important we let people make these decisions for themselves," she's saying, but amid my desire to manage the tension in the room I'm not entirely focused on what she's going on to explain. (Concision is not one of Charlotte's strong points.) I hear her go on a while before she concludes, "It's not right to tell other people what to do." I can't tell whether she's making a general statement or reacting directly to Amir. Normally I might ask her, but I'm a little afraid of the direction this conversation is taking. In any case, Evan is looking at me expectantly. I nod to him.

"I think we're mixing up two different questions here," he says evenly, though his eyes betray intensity, even anger. "Whether or not people marry and whether they have children are two different things. But I don't think it's right to refer to anybody as a 'mistake.'"

Evan's remark hangs in the air. Amir is looking straight ahead: he has no interest in a rejoinder. Nor does anyone else want to wade into this one. I glance up at the clock. A few minutes to go. I'm going to bail. "All right then," I say. "This has been a good discussion. For tomorrow, I'd like you to read . . ."

As is my custom, when class is over I open the door, put down the doorstop, and see students off individually, like a pastor at his church. Evan, who's seated next to the exit, is the first to leave. "Thank you, Evan," I say, "I appreciated your remarks today."

"Thanks, Mr. D," he says. He's trying—I'm moved by his commitment to maintaining an even temperament—but the strain is there. "See you tomorrow," he says as he sweeps by, and his place is taken by the procession of his classmates. Sorry, I want to say. It wasn't supposed to go like this. But I don't.

🎕🎕

Diversity: it's been the defining term for those of us who came of age in the closing decades of the twentieth century. For some it's a steady process of social transformation; for others, a rallying cry with which to quicken the pace of change. For others still, diversity is an established reality. At any given moment, diversity can be any of these for the same person. But its centrality in our public discourse is in any event difficult to question. No one, after all, hears "unity" invoked with the same ideological fervor that one hears about diversity. Even those who don't like it rarely say so directly.

Actually, *diversity* (and its close cousin *inclusion*) has largely supplanted another term — *integration* — that was at the center of national discourse in the mid-twentieth century. In part, *integration* has faded as a key term because with the passage of time it seemed to imply a little too much sameness, not enough recognition or accommodation of difference, for the people who once championed it. So it is that the tides of opinion change over time. For better or worse, there's likely to come a time when *unity*, or some word like it, really does come into vogue.

Diversity is a term that often engenders impatience: depending on whom you ask, there's almost always too much or too little of it. There is also ongoing debate — and disagreement — over what it actually means. Supporter and critic alike will often presume, without saying so directly, that diversity is primarily a matter of race and that *race* is a code term for "African American," which is a kind of gold standard for diversity in American society given the undeniable — but variously interpreted — legacy of slavery in US history. Depending on the circumstances, and for opposing reasons, supporter and critic alike will also push back against the idea that diversity = black, noting that racial diversity includes other people, too. And that it means something beyond race — diversity includes categories of gender, and class, and, apropos of the current discussion, mental and physical disabilities.

For the most part, I have fairly conventional opinions about diversity for someone of my demographic and generation. At a minimum I accept it, and in some circumstances I actively champion it, though my identity as an able-bodied white man inevitably raises questions about the depth of my understanding and ardor in the matter. I've listened to my fair share of consultants explain that the learning process should offer a mirror as well as a window to students, and I take that to heart. I also wonder whether it's possible to move on from there.

There is one aspect of diversity that I think tends to get short shrift in these discussions: diversity of opinion. That's not especially surprising; birds of an ideological feather flock together. The reasons are understandable, even good, ranging from a desire to minimize friction to the sense of clarity, even depth, that can come into focus when the people who are discussing an issue or problem share premises or commitments. That said, I tend to agree with the remark of twentieth-century journalist Walter Lippmann, who once reputedly said, "When everybody thinks alike, nobody thinks very much."

To that end, I'm always on the lookout for opportunities to challenge student assumptions. So I'll question the prevailing liberal common sense that we need more gun control (even though I share that view) by noting that the United States has always been a gun culture, and indeed without widespread ownership of guns in the eighteenth century there never would have been an American Revolution. When a student says people who feel abortions are wrong shouldn't have them, I say people who think owning slaves is wrong shouldn't buy them. But conversations like these always seem to founder on the irreconcilable divide on whether, in the latter case, a woman's fertilized egg is a human being. The Cleopatra Society simulation is my attempt to find my way out of this cul de sac and take things in a potentially useful direction.

I'm aware, though, that in formulating this attempt to complicate the prevailing orthodoxy surrounding diversity, I'm also wading into potentially problematic territory involving another buzz term in educational discourse: *safety*. Schools need to be safe spaces, we're told. The domain of this injunction is wide, ranging from landscaping considerations to antibullying initiatives to sensitivity training in matters of identity politics. As a practical matter, you can't really be against safety. Yet its very totalizing quality makes me skeptical, even at times hostile. Safety insulates, even suffocates.

Sure, kids who live in fear can't learn. But learning without risks is barely learning at all. No pain, no gain. I'm not sure how far I want to go with this. But there's something — I can't quite tell if it's a strength or a weakness — that instinctively impels me to push back against conventional wisdom.

⁂

Dennis Farnsworth pokes his head in my door. "Horace," he says. "Got a minute?"

Dennis is the tenth-grade dean. He's been at it a long time, a true master of a job that has loads of accountability but relatively little administrative power: supervising a grade of kids.

"It's about Evan," he says, sitting down.

"I was afraid you were going to say that."

"So you know."

"We had a tough discussion in class yesterday," I tell him. "I felt badly about it."

"I of course don't know exactly what happened," he replies. "I only know what Evan tells me. And what Evan tells me is that his feelings were hurt. And that it was you that hurt his feelings."

I repeat him neutrally: "I hurt his feelings."

"Yes. In Evan's words: 'I can't believe Mr. Dewey didn't speak up. Why didn't he speak out against what Amir said?'"

I nod. After a pause, I say, "I didn't think it would be a good idea to shut Amir down. I don't think he understood the implications of what he was saying. But silencing him just didn't seem like a good idea in that moment. To be honest with you, it still doesn't. It's only when you actually say those things, try them out and get a reaction, that you really begin to understand what they mean."

Now it's Dennis who nods. "I understand. You're Amir's teacher, too."

"Exactly."

"And Evan's. That's why I thought you should know."

"I'll talk to him."

"No," Dennis says. "You can't do that. I actually suggested that Evan go to you, but he said 'Absolutely not.'" He shakes his head. "I don't know why he was so adamant about that, but he was. I'm engaging in a little bit of duplicity here, Horace, because Evan never actually said 'Don't tell Mr. Dewey,' but it's my guess that if I asked that's exactly what he would say. I'm making the calculation that you should be aware of where he is and calibrate the best you can. I'm not all that worried about Evan, in that he's a resilient kid who's dealt with a whole lot worse than this. Actually, I'm glad he felt he could blow off some steam with me. But it would be a real problem if he knew we had this conversation."

"Understood, Dennis. Thank you."

Dennis pats me on the shoulder before he heads out. "Sounds like a hell of a class," he says. "You're really pushing the envelope there, Horace. What's the name of that book — *The Blessing of a Skinned Knee?* I get it. But try to keep a first aid kit on hand, OK?"

"Yessir," I say, feeling a little bit like Dennis is giving me a friendly shove on the way out the door. I think he thinks I should ditch this whole Cleopatra Society thing. He might be right. But I'm not yet ready to give it up.

PROJECTION

When my wife drops me off at the corner of Second Avenue and 125th Street, I shed my first layer of unease: the fact that she's the one who's brought me here. This is something I should have been able to manage on my own. But the fact of the matter is that I have a phobia about Manhattan driving, and the last time I tried to overcome it by driving my son's friend home from a soccer game on Randall's Island, I got in a fender-bender with a taxi driver on Park Avenue and 76th. So when I complain about the train schedule over lunch on the shared Tuesday of our spring break, she insists she has the time to swing me down to PS 411, an offer I accept sheepishly. Still, I note as we arrive, a trip that would have taken an hour via public transportation takes only about twenty-five minutes in midday traffic (though I later learn she hits bridge traffic on the way back).

Watching her drive away, I turn my attention to my other sources of unease. Though I know this part of Manhattan—just like every other part of the island—has been gentrifying, I still have childhood associations with it as a dangerous area, a feeling that gets reinforced now when I see how wide and empty 125th Street is at this end, which seems vaguely threatening even on a sunny March afternoon. Another feeling, which kicks in as I begin walking down a somewhat more crowded First Avenue, is guilt: I feel like I'm trespassing. A middle-aged white man is in a decided minority in these precincts, and while no one gives me hostile looks (or, for that matter, seems especially surprised to see me), I still feel like I'm violating rules that seem no less valid for being unwritten. But a third—and increasingly strong—emotion I'm experiencing is anger: *C'mon, Horace. Every day hundreds of children at the school I'm visiting walk these streets, and if they have any trepidation in doing so it's hardly something they can do much about.* I see the entrance across the street and make my way past windows covered by a chain link fence into the lobby.

I'm visiting at the invitation of Carson Beck, the dynamo founder of PS 411 as well as a half-dozen other schools across the neighborhood. I knew nothing about her before getting her e-mail six weeks earlier—"We're looking for someone to join our team who has experience teaching history and mentoring history teachers," she wrote—but in the time since I'd read a fair amount, including a *New York Times* story about charter school controversies I'd encountered over breakfast a few days later. I was loosely familiar with the issues surrounding schools like 411; at their best they offered a combination of innovation and accountability to quality-starved families, though there were questions about equity in terms of siphoning off the best students from the public school system, and about their penchant for relying on wealthy philanthropists who were perceived to be using schools as a means of advancing a libertarian social agenda. (Beck herself had been a hedge fund manager who cashed out before the crash and decided to turn her attention to advancing public education.)

What makes Beck's charter schools a little unusual is that they're avowedly progressive. Conventional wisdom held that the most successful startup schools are run on a conservative model—uniforms, tightly regimented routines, a skill-and-drill approach to testing essential to meeting state mandates. The Beck website noted that all its schools met proficiency standards and that 100 percent of the previous year's high school class graduated. The problem, from what I understand, is teacher turnover. Charter schools tend to chew up young teachers. And I've come across blog comments that suggest Carson Beck in particular can be a stern taskmaster. But there's no sign of that on the website or in my communications with her. "We're ready to take the next step," Carson's e-mail had said. "And that's why we're turning to you."

I had responded positively to her overture, which she made in January. But it wasn't until early March when she called to follow up, apologizing for what she described as a series of distractions. Was I still willing to pay a visit? Unclear about what she had in mind, but sufficiently intrigued to think it was worth the experience even if nothing further came of it, I agreed to make the trip to East Harlem during my coming break.

Now I stand in the lobby of the building, bright in the afternoon light but dilapidated, presided over by a security guard behind a desk. I explain my business and she sends me sent to the fourth floor, one of two occupied by PS 411. (Another charter school inhabits the other two floors; though I'd heard such arrangements were commonplace, it still seems strange to imagine multiple schools in the same building.) The stairwells are wide but dark, the glazed walls an ugly mustard brick. I poke my head into a cluttered teacher's resource room, where a young woman directs me down the hall to Carson's assistant, Enrique Leval, who is apparently to serve as my minder. Enrique, who appears to be a few years shy of thirty, is a light-skinned Latino with a ponytail and a manner I associate with Wesleyan or Oberlin (I later learn he is a graduate of Pomona). "Carson is meeting with one of our trustees," he explains apologetically. "She'll be available in a few minutes. In the meantime, I'll show you around."

I notice the hallway — this part of it for fifth graders — is covered with student work, along with posters bearing messages like "You Can Do It!" and "A Dream is a Wish Your Heart Makes!" The effect is cheerful despite the dim lighting. Yet I somehow feel a sense of strain, like a forced smile. Is this just me projecting? Apparently so: I'm still trying to process my impressions while listening to Enrique when a bell rings and students begin cascading out of classrooms into the hallway, their chatter cheerfully animated. "Hi Mr. Leval!" a chorus of voices says. I'm a little startled when I see a series of brown faces look me right in the eye and smile. They're so openhearted.

Enrique reaches into his pocket and glances at his phone. "She's ready," he says to me, his pace quickening as we head toward a staircase. He tells me he met Carson when she made a fundraising trip to California last year. She recruited him to be an assistant principal at 411. He seems impossibly young for such responsibility, but I guess this is one strategy for innovating on a shoestring. He leads me to what looks like a surprisingly improvised office—a secretary at an old desk, bookshelves supported on milk crates on either side of her. "Go right in," she says to us, motioning beyond the wall to Enrique. I decline an offer of a bottle of water.

"Hello!" Carson says, getting up from her desk, which sits beside a large window looking out onto First Avenue. The office has the feel of a stylish, spacious grad-student apartment furnished à la IKEA. This is clearly a statement; Carson, who I'm guessing lives on dividend income, wants to work simply. But her couture is another matter. While there's nothing overtly flashy about it—white blouse, black pants and boots—a silver bracelet, diamond wedding ring, and expensive haircut radiate good taste. She's north of fifty but looks younger, her skin flawless. "I'm so glad we're finally meeting," she says, as if our encounter were the culmination of overcome obstacles.

Her secretary calls to her from the other side of the wall that Henry is on the phone. "Tell him I'm on my way," she says, a faint trace of irritation in her voice. "Tell him I'll be downtown in twenty minutes." I can't decide whether to be more amused or dismayed by this lie. Guess this will be a short meeting.

"So: East Hudson!" Carson says, turning her attention back to me. "I hear such great things." She proceeds to tell me something about how her sister's best friend went to East Hudson in the late eighties, and how her husband's business partner is a trustee, and lots of other patter that gets punctuated by my confessing I don't know the people she's talking about until she finally mentions an alum I taught a decade ago. We agree he's wonderful. Another phone call, this one from someone named Randall. Carson ponders this for a moment. "Not now," she says. "I'll call him back when I'm headed downtown."

She glances at a brass clock on her desk. "Damn," she says aloud to herself, before looking at me. "I'm really sorry about this," she says. "I'm going to have to run. But that's all right, because I've designated Enrique here to be your host. He's going to take you to a few classes so that you can get a feel for the place. Then we can have a talk about where we might go from there. Just tell me one thing: how might you go about joining our new progressive teaching institute? I'm planning to launch one next year, and I'm looking for a history educator to round out my roster."

This is a curveball. Is she disorganized, or is she testing me? I want to pause to collect my thoughts, but I'm aware of that clock. I begin talking about things like workshops on the use of primary sources, essay fundamentals, and lesson planning. I manage to use the phrases "collaborative learning" and "student-centered," feeling a little like I'm bullshitting, because while I believe in this stuff and do it to greater or lesser degrees, I rarely use such language.

Carson is listening to me very closely, her attention alternately flattering and disconcerting. I pause and she nods. "Yes. That sounds very promising." She looks sharply at Enrique. "Take Mr. Dewey up to Stella's class," she tells him. "I want him to see what she's doing. The writing stuff is very important." As she speaks she's gathering her handbag and reaching for her coat. She beams at me as she puts on her coat. "This has been a real pleasure!" Her secretary comes in bearing a bottle of water that she grabs without looking at her.

We're accompanying her to the doorway when we hear a voice: "Hi, Mrs. Beck!"

"Jonquil!" Carson replies, stroking a pretty girl's face. "How are you, sweetheart?"

"Fine."

"And how is your sister?"

"Fine."

"Well, you say hello to her for me. And your mom, too."

"I will."

Carson looks back at me for the final time. "Thanks so much for coming," she says. "We'll be in touch." With that she heads downstairs.

Enrique looks at me neutrally. Is he sizing me up? (Is he the reason, I will wonder later, why this is the last I ever hear about a progressive teaching institute—or from Carson Beck?) "Shall we proceed?" he asks. I nod, and we begin walking in the other direction. "We're going to go to Stella Levine's eighth-grade class," he explains.

When we enter the classroom at the other end of the hall, I'm struck by how full it is: there are a good thirty kids in here, about twice my typical load. A slightly overweight white teacher in her thirties stands in front of the room next to a state-of-the-art Smart Board, with an assistant teacher (tall, Afro, maybe twenty-five) in the back. The Smart Board is projecting a headline I can see from where I'm standing: "The Power of Two." I recognize this as the title of a recent book about creative partnerships. I'm surprised and impressed. "All right, then?" she asks the students. "Mr. Medrano and myself will be walking around the room helping you. So take ten minutes to answer the leading question in your journals."

She looks over at Enrique and me and smiles. "Mr. Leval," she says affectionately. "To what do I owe the honor?" The assistant teacher, Medrano, looks over at us guardedly, but I can't tell what the source of his suspicion is (me?).

"This is Horace Dewey," Enrique explains.

"Ah, East Hudson," she nods appreciatively as he explains my background and why I'm there. "Well, Theo and I were just going to work the room. Why don't you join us?"

Enrique nods and looks at me. "Yeah, sure," I say. *Oh no*, I think.

I make my way to the far side of the room, looking for a safe harbor. There in the second row I see a boy staring at the Smart Board intently. He's large for his age, with bluish-black skin. I crouch next to him and gaze at the board, feeling a chair materialize behind me: Theo has set me up. "Friendship is an important source of power," I read out loud as I settle into the chair. "Martin Luther King Jr. depended on his friend Ralph Abernathy when they worked together to lead the civil rights movement." (There's a picture of the two standing side by side in a moment of levity.) "Describe a friendship in your life and why it's important." I pause to look at the boy again, who faces me for the first time. I can see the outlines of the handsome man he'll become, but they're still soft. I can't quite read his expression and am unsettled by the fact that he doesn't seem to find my presence at all strange. "Do you have a friendship in mind?" I ask by way of an opening gambit.

"My father," he says, confusing me.

"You're friends with your father?"

"My father," he repeats. "My father got hurt."

"Your father got hurt?"

"Yeah. His friend."

"Your father got hurt by his friend?" Half of me is appalled by this child's apparent difficulty with basic communication, and the other half appalled by my inability to lock in on a wavelength, something I've always thought of myself as reasonably good at.

"Yeah. Hurt."

"Was this a close friend?"

"Yeah."

I wonder if I should ask what happened. I'm struck by the undercurrent of vehemence in his voice; he seems angered on his father's behalf. Am I right to hear love there? I feel like I'm trying to understand someone who's speaking a foreign language from facial expressions and inflection, and am embarrassed by having to resort to this: I really should know better.

"What do you think it means to be a friend?" I ask him.

"It means you're with somebody. Loyal."

"Yes, I can see that. Maybe you can write some of this down?"

He nods. He turns his gaze to the spiral notebook in front of him, picks up a pencil, and begins to write. How long will this make sense to him? This kid still seems to think there's some relationship between what goes on in a classroom and what goes on in his life. I see plenty of kids at my school who stop believing it to be the case, though they can usually get away with this loss of faith and muddle through to graduation. According to the numbers at PS 411, this kid will graduate, too. That seems a little hard to believe. I so wish I could say something, do something, that would be useful to him. But I've got no magic here.

I feel Enrique tap my shoulder. "We've got to go," he says.

I get up and put my hand on the boy's shoulder. "Keep working on this," I tell him. "Maybe you can tell your dad how you feel." He nods without looking up, continuing to write on the page.

Over the course of the next hour or so, we visit three more rooms, and I sit in on a workshop session where a group of young teachers are talking about students as well as engaging matters of craft. "Really terrific stuff," I tell Enrique, and he nods as if it's a matter of course. He says a few more things about the summer institute — still talking to people, hoping to finalize — and agrees to follow up. We exchange notes of mutual thanks by e-mail the following day.

I leave PS 411 as school ends, cheerful throngs spilling out onto the sidewalk, where a row of buses waits. I walk amid a cluster of kids back up First Avenue, making a left on 125th Street. It seems less menacing now, particularly as I head west and can see the Metro North station in the distance (my wife and I agreed I would take the train back). As I walk past a collection of used bathtubs for sale on the sidewalk — *huh?* — I decide something has to come of this, and I'm hoping that maybe I can get involved with PS 411 in some modest way. But I also remember last week's faculty meeting, where the director of diversity for the high school described a summer program for students at academic risk, especially minority students entering East Hudson in ninth grade, who may not have been socialized for a prep school environment. Maybe I can do something there. But Jesus, I've got a lot to learn.

ENLARGING THE WORLD

There's an expectant air as I enter the humid auditorium for the last assembly of the school year. That's because today, June 1, is the day of the Senior Video. A beach ball bounces from chair to chair, an element of boisterousness that would not be acceptable under other circumstances, but as this is the last time the seniors will be with us—we can't very well suspend them at this point—such laxity must be tolerated. In any case, we don't really have to worry about discipline problems on a day like today; the younger kids cheer the seniors on because they know they're seniors in the making. Everyone is eager for the proceedings to begin.

Hannah Osborne is addressing the gathered throng—students in their seats, teachers milling in the aisles, and school head Alan Sanders standing in the back with his arms folded. "We gather to observe one of our most cherished customs," she's telling the students. "The Senior Video committee has been working for months to record a year in the life in the history of the school. So without further ado let me welcome the leaders of that committee, Sammy Inohofe and Derian Semple-Weiss!"

A roar of applause accompanies Sammy and Derian as they take the stage, followed by chants of "Seniors! *Seniors!*" I don't really know Derian—she's seemed like a nice kid from afar, a cousin of my student Dana Weiss—but Sammy irritates me. Once again, he's missed an essay deadline, this one his final project for the semester. If I'd wanted to get in his face, I could have prevented this moment of triumph, since the school's

151

policy is that all senior work was to have been finished by now and he could essentially have been held hostage until it was finished. Of course if we enforced that policy at least a third of the grade would be under some form of academic probation. Still, I could probably get away with enforcing it with Sammy, because he's an entitled brat who has likely never considered the way he has routinely inconvenienced my colleagues and me with his cavalier attitude about things like getting to class before attendance gets taken, turning in work without having to be nagged, and the like. I'd be surprised that none of my colleagues blocked his path if I wasn't confident that he's gamed us in one way or another.

So it is that he stands before his peers, basking in their attention. "OK, you guys," Derien is saying, "we have a lot of people to thank." As she reads from a lengthy list, Sammy is hailing his buddies like a presidential candidate after a debate. As she finishes, he almost cuts her off: "But of course the most important people we need to thank are the *seniors!*" (Much clapping and shouting.) "This is our show. *This is how we roll!*" As soon as he says it, the lights go down and the video begins to project.

The video opens with a scene of a classroom with six students, five of whom I recognize. "Well, people," Sammy is saying from the front of the room with Derian beside him, "the Senior Video assembly is tomorrow and we have a severe lack of footage. What are we going to do?"

"I think we should try and feature the history and science departments," Ebony Reynolds says with an earnestness that's clearly ironic. "The faculty feel — "

"Let me stop you right there," Sammy says, cutting her off. "That's a terrible idea." The camera shoots back to Ebony, who bears an exaggerated frown. Lots of guffaws from the crowd.

"We need spectacle," Lorrie Menand says.

"Trucks, trains, explosions," adds Steve Enright.

"Breathtaking, magical, nostalgic," Bess Cimini says with over-the-top earnestness. "And arts and crafts."

The kid I don't know utters a word that gets bleeped out. Derian has been scribbling all this down on the blackboard, but we can't see what she's just written, which is part of the joke.

"Call me old-fashioned," Julia Aikman says, "but I think this senior video should go back to the beginning. The rafting trip we took as a grade at the end of last summer." Suddenly there's a screen fade to black, the music of "Wipeout" comes up, and we're off: another Senior Video is under way. I sit restlessly in the dark, torn between my desire to leave and my curiosity about who—and what—will matter. Though I already know what won't.

❧❦❧

One thing you never get from a senior video is an affirmation of the life of the mind—the value of ideas for their own sake, not as a matter of a diploma or a job but as propositions that enrich everyday experience and inform long-term goals the way schooling occasionally does. There will sometimes be a scene in a senior video with a classroom setting, which is almost always silly. It's not impossible to imagine a routine with real substance—a playful commentary on the periodic table, for example, or an allegorical poem commenting on the nature of schooling. Or maybe just a kid reflecting on a memorable lesson she learned in a course. Something that suggests that what happened in the classroom has been absorbed and deployed in a meaningful way outside it. I can't recall anything like that in fifteen years of watching these the videos.

I realize this may sound like an unrealistic, even stupid, lament. A senior video by definition is a student-centered document; you can't expect the things a teacher considers important to be the same things a student considers important. The classroom is your chosen domain; what you see in a video is theirs: their classmates, their rituals—their *time*—memorialized.

But I'm not actually (well, not primarily) making a lament. Instead, I'm identifying a core reality for any teacher entering a school setting: the academic dimension of schooling is really a relatively small part of a student's life. The intellectual dimension, which is by no means the same thing, is even smaller. Whether or not students or faculty are consciously aware of this truth, it shapes their mutual expectations and experiences.

That the life of the mind plays a relatively small role in the experience of high school is a little counterintuitive. Certainly the majority of time that a student spends on a campus on any given day is in a classroom. As substantial as that can be, though, class time must be considered in the context of other activities, not just practice or rehearsal but also travel time to and from school, passing time between classes (which can really add up over the course of a day), lunchtime, study halls, assemblies, and the like.

Further, class time is divided into segments of relatively short duration. A student spends more time in class *as a whole* than anywhere else, but usually less than an hour in any given class on any given day, notwithstanding a science lab maybe once a week or the occasional extended period that a block schedule permits. By contrast, the same student may spend hours a day on an athletic field, in a rehearsal space, or at a social setting in the school. Students may have hours of homework, but they're typically splintered by subject and undertaken in a context in which music listening, text messaging, and any number of other interruptions, welcome or not, are taking place. Even the best and most committed students face real challenges in achieving the sustained focus that's a prerequisite for achievement in any field, let alone academic ones.

The time that students spend in the classroom is also inevitably going to vary in quality—some teachers are better than others, some classes are better organized than others, and some sections of the same course have a better interpersonal chemistry than others even when the subject and teacher is the same. Nor are students the only issue here. Indeed, teachers can get so habituated to their routines, and harried by the cycle of deadlines in the school year, that they can lose touch with their intellectual passions. Amid tasks like taking attendance, managing grades, and attending meetings, it often seems that the job of being a teacher has relatively little to do with academic substance.

But even a teacher on top of her game is at best only half the equation. Few people of any age or background can consistently focus for twenty minutes at time, never mind forty or fifty. Some students are incorrigibly sociable; others will drift mentally without even realizing they're doing it. On any given day romances will be in the process of being made or broken, athletic glory or disaster will loom, the last party or the next one will be a subject of gossip. And all of this is separate from the medical question of the degree to which the ability to pay attention is, or should be, a matter of pharmacological treatment. There are students with undiagnosed attention deficit disorders, others who abuse drugs, and still others who have benefited from treatment but face additional obstacles. The fact that *anything* gets learned sometimes seems miraculous.

Of course, the life of the mind has always been a minority

pursuit. Those who commit to it are always on the lookout for each other, and there are few more satisfying experiences than an encounter between the hungry student eager for guidance and the hopeful teacher eager to share what she knows — or wonders about. Part of what makes this exciting is that it doesn't happen all that often.

And that's because the life of the mind — which, whatever else may be going on in the job, must be the pilot light of the living teacher — is only one of many minority pursuits with legitimate charm. (There are also those with illegitimate charm that provide even tougher competition.) To greater or lesser degrees, students will be beguiled by the bright lights of stardom and dreams whose plausibility is uncertain at best. And yet for that very reason, some will instinctively seek an alternative, sooner or later and for greater or lesser stretches of time. As a teacher, you have the job of biding your time for those who are ready and willing to come your way.

Amid all the obstacles that stand in your path in such an enterprise, you have one crucial asset working in your favor even with those who are not kindred spirits. Which is that some part of your students will root for you, if for no other reason than that they don't want to be bored. They may not show this bias in your favor; they may not even fully know they have it, and in any case you can lose them with breathtaking speed. But among the deepest longings of an adolescent is to see old people who are reasonably happy with what they're doing, so that they can imagine becoming reasonably happy old people themselves, even if they have no intention of ever becoming teachers. They're instinctive collectors of such scenarios; the more they have, the more confident they'll be that there are many avenues in which to pursue happiness. They want the world to be that much bigger. That's really what a good teacher does: enlarge the world.

How do you go about the business of enlarging the world? If you're a history teacher, at least, the first step is helping students understand how weird they are. How much they are creatures of their moment, their common sense as yesterday's heresy and tomorrow's myth. Students tend to assume others have the same motivations they do, typically cast in terms of self-interest rightly understood, overlooking how difficult it can be to determine what one's self-interest actually *is*. (Would *you* have bet against Hitler in June of 1940?) My goal is to give them a sense of contingency: to show them one can have very different assumptions from the ones that govern their own lives; that those assumptions result in reasoning that leads in alternative directions; and that those directions lead to very different outcomes.

This is the work of the classroom. More specifically, it's the work of teachers — something that neither books nor computers, nor any of the other tools or methods we associate with learning can accomplish. It's the teacher who teases propositions out, not simply by telling students what they need to know but by patiently querying them, asking open-ended questions that are not experienced as steering toward a predetermined outcome, but rather as expressions of curiosity that invite comparison with the ideas and guesses of other people in the room (it's here that the much-invoked ideal of diversity comes to life). You want students to experience their own particularity — and a sense of variety they may not have known, much less suspected, among their peers.

But the real trick is to get them *beyond* that — to learn to see others as something more than, something *in addition to*, means of appreciating themselves. That means trying to understand not only their peers, or the teacher leading the discussion, or their parents, but human beings in other times and places. That's what education finally is: an act of imagination.

And, just maybe, an act of empathy. But this is an even bigger stretch. As earnestly as we try to teach students to care about others, this is not something we can really count on, especially since we're fitful at best in doing it ourselves. To me, this is one of the more haunting aspects of being a teacher: I'm not confident that it's made me a better person. Or, if it has, I still come up so far short. If nothing else, I'd like to believe that living so much inside my own head has given me an appreciation of the limits of ideas—that they don't necessarily change interests, and that there's more to life than mere ideas. This is why I've come to appreciate what I think of as wonderful temperaments—those students and faculty whose good cheer and goodwill seem like a form of intelligence in its own right. There are some kids whose smiles, conferred with wonderful ingenuousness, are so instinctive and free of calculation that I experience them as a gift.

I lack such qualities. But having them is not finally indispensable to my job as I understand it (though these qualities are what makes some teachers successful, particularly at the elementary level). My job as a history teacher is to make the world a bigger place by introducing the student to other people, some of whom happen to be dead, and make those students aware that their circumstances are, for better and worse, hardly the only, and certainly not a permanent, outcome. You do that right and everyday life becomes a drama at least as compelling as a senior video.

❀❦❀

We've hit all the highlights—Pajama Day, Halloween, the athletic triumphs, the spring musical. The footage of our seniors back when they were little kids—some of it is uncanny in capturing the unchanging essence of these kids. (Robbie Menzies's grin has not changed a whit since he was four years old.) There was also the skit in which Hannah presided over a hearing in which Alberto Mores was disciplined for his failure to return student essays within four years of receiving them. ("Oh, I'll get to them," Alberto promises, good-naturedly accepting an unsubtle critique of a well-known bad habit—one that probably should not be a joking matter for Hannah, though I'm inclined to make allowances for her the way she does for him.) There was also a silent slideshow tribute to Marybeth Ianuzzi, currently in hospice treatment; I'm told the end is near. I think it would have been better if faculty and students had spoken to and about Marybeth—she's not dead yet—but maybe that would have been just too hard.

Now the senior dean, Letty Aronson, is saying all the usual things: this has been a special class, their legacy will be powerful and lasting, and similarly comforting lies. Being able to say such things with conviction is probably one of the job requirements for a dean—that and endless patience, which is why I will never be one.

I look at my watch: 10:16. They've got less than three minutes to finish—Hannah will have already previewed it and made sure it came in under an hour—and it's clear they're going to the last second. We're back in the classroom where the whole video started. "What are we going to do, Sammy?" Derian asks in a plaintive wail. "We have nothing to work with!"

"Nonsense," a serenely confident Sammy replies. "We'll just wing it."

"How are we going to do that? Sammy, don't you understand how serious this is!"

The camera zooms in on Sammy's face. He winks. "We'll just show everybody breaking out of school. The ultimate happy ending."

An abrupt cut to the backdoor of the gym. We begin hearing that pop hit song that uses Pachelbel's Canon ("Friends Forever," I think it's called). Suddenly—well, no, not suddenly, because everything is in slow motion—the double doors open. And through them spills wave after wave of the senior class. Debbie Godlowski. Evan Beckwith. Janice Vennnerman. That kid with the silly crewcut—Josh something or other. Each of them looks almost impossibly happy—maybe because they're being directed to look that way, or because they really are happy, or some combination of the two. Laura Johnson's long hair streams behind her. Becky Robison's boobs bob. Bill Fox's baseball cap looks like it might fly off, but doesn't while he's still in the frame. The cumulative effect of this youthful vitality moves, even awes, me. They look so eager and confident to face the world—my God, even dour Gina Bernstein is smiling. I spend so much time trying to mold and challenge their energy—begrudging them their energy and not enough simply savoring it.

Will some of these happy faces end up disappointed? Count on it. Will Sammy Inohofe remain a jerk? Bet my bottom dollar. But right now, the world is plenty big enough. They have hope. And for the moment, so do I.

AMONG PARENTS

PARENTAL TEACHING

෴

I'm in the middle of something I'd hoped to avoid: a face-to-face conversation with a parent. "I had number of questions after last night's open house," Erica Champlain had e-mailed a few days earlier. "I would appreciate it if we could schedule a meeting. Please let me know when would be good."

I tried to parry this, forfeiting my default suggestion of e-mail in the hope of compromise: "Perhaps we could confer by phone, whereby it may be possible to address your questions sooner?"

Nothing doing. "I'd like to talk about Kevin's learning issues. So I think a face-to-face meeting will make that a little easier," she replied.

"Easier for whom?" I muttered under my breath as I sent along some proposed times.

Like most of my colleagues, I'm not always opposed to meeting with parents, something that happens less often in secondary schools than at the primary level. Indeed, there are times when teachers will actively solicit such conferences. But in general there's an unofficial friction built into the parent-teacher relationship comparable to that of the teacher-administrator relationship. Though we all presumably have the same goal—what's best for the child—our respective roles can us lead to different, and sometimes conflicting, perspectives on what that actually means. We all know this, and proceed to act as if we don't.

This meeting is pretty much going the way I thought it would. Erica is attractive, polite, and elegant, her good manners not entirely concealing a combination of steeliness and unease (which I attribute to her presence on my turf and her concerns about her child—not necessarily in that order). "Thank you for meeting with me," she says, a good opening move as I bid her to sit.

I counter with a query about traffic, and we comment on the weather before I get down to business: "So what can I do for you?"

What follows is a biography. Smart child, deeply committed. But one who has always struggled. Tested for learning disabilities, now entitled to extra time for tests, has regular appointments with the school's learning specialists. And private tutors (now a standard accessory for students of means). Last year's history teacher not as good as the year before—that teacher was wonderful—but they all got through it. This year Kevin is excited, he's heard good things about my class, but it just moves so *fast*. Lots of anxiety about the essay Kevin has just turned in. Erica is uneasy because she isn't aware that there's actually a curriculum map in my department, and, well, there seem to be inconsistencies in teacher expectations from year to year and between departments. *Curriculum map*: she knows the jargon, which she deploys to convey that she's a savvy advocate on her child's behalf.

Erica goes on for a while, and since she's thorough—and since I don't actually hear a question—I remain silent, my mind wandering from the price of her shoes to the image of her sitting beside Kevin at the dining room table as he does homework. (One version of this features a shouting match; another is a scene of quiet amity—I don't doubt the depth of this mother's love for her child and the positive results it has yielded.) My attention gets refocused when she states, "I know you're not going to change the way you teach," even as I know that at some level this is exactly what she wants me to do. In the most general terms, that means giving her kid more personalized attention, which I'm willing to do, though I doubt that will be to the extent and with the degree of explicit commitment that she wants from me.

The pause that follows tells me that it's my turn to talk. I tell Erica that I understand her concerns and that I have no wish to trivialize or dismiss them. I also tell her that on the basis of what I've seen — a kid who got a C– on his first test and a B– on that essay, which I invited him to revise and which, at his initiative, we've scheduled a meeting to discuss this very afternoon — I'm not worried about Kevin's ability to keep pace, even thrive, in my course. I realize that Kevin, who has occasionally raised his hand in class to make a relevant comment, is not exactly sailing through it with flying colors. But in that regard he's hardly alone. There are many students in the course who get off to a tentative start, stabilize, and improve, and I see no reason to think that won't be true here.

I realize as I say this that I'm not telling Erica what she wants to hear. For one thing, I'm lumping her child in with a bunch of other kids. For another, I seem to be telling her that mediocrity is acceptable. In preparation for this meeting, I took a look at Kevin's transcript and saw that his grades were quite good, ranging from B+ to A. I suspect that's the result of a good deal of sweat equity, and perhaps some lobbying of the kind I'm experiencing here. Am I telling her that this approach isn't going to work anymore? Maybe. A hard message, and one that under other circumstances I might feel more squeamish about delivering. But I'm acting on the belief that controlled candor, if I can maintain it, is the most educational thing, in the broadest sense of that term, I can deliver. But I need to maintain my concentration.

Erica, in any case, is not willing to conclude our meeting, and at this point she makes more specific queries directed to my practices in particular. Kevin had trouble with the test, she explains, because I didn't provide a review sheet. That's correct. I regard it as important that students begin to absorb and synthesize information themselves. Standardized tests are coming, et cetera.

"That's kinda tough so early in the year. Couldn't there be some kind of middle ground?"

"There is. All my lecture notes are online. By at least some standards that counts as a study guide."

"What about review time? Do you put aside time to go over the test?"

"Yes." At this point, perhaps unnecessarily, I play a card I've been holding in reserve: "There were a number of students who performed very well on the test. I regard it as part of my job to craft assessments that evoke a range of performance."

Erica nods grimly; she knows.

She takes another tack. The zero-to-sixty quality of the test also seemed to characterize my approach to the first essay, she says. In previous years Kevin's teachers spelled out the intermediate steps. Is there some plan, some sequence to the expectations, like there was with that fabulous teacher a couple years ago? Is this something I would be willing to lay out for him?

I agree that the other teacher is fabulous (and implicitly suggest that I'm content to be a good deal less fabulous). I also say that writing instruction is taken very seriously at this school. Faculty in individual departments confer, different departments confer, and teachers in different grades confer. I pull out a book I use on writing instruction. She looks it over noncommittally. While she does I explain that one of the challenges we face is that kids are all over the map developmentally. Some tenth graders come in capable of college-level work. Others will graduate with limited skills that may or may not improve. Girls tend to be better than boys at this stage of the game. Erica nods: yes, she knows that too. I explain that I will work with students on an ad hoc basis and provide specific encouragement and any needed direction in the work they produce, as indeed I'll be doing later that day. There are particular criteria I use to judge any given essay: the presence and clarity of a thesis; strong topic sentences; adequate evidence; awareness of counterarguments; and so on. But I'm not going to commit myself to enumerating these every time I meet with an individual student.

"The fact that some kids struggle is not a sign that something is wrong," I conclude, aware that she thinks I'm talking at her. "Actually, it may well be that something is right: education often is a product of struggle."

Once more, Erica nods, lips pursed. It looks like she wishes it just didn't have to be so damn hard.

Erica's arsenal is exhausted: I'm a brick wall, and I'm not crumbling. I'd be lying if I didn't confess to a measure of satisfaction in this—teachers no less than parents come to these sessions with a measure of defensiveness, and this woman has shown herself to be a worthy adversary, even if I still feel, as I have all along, that there's something unseemly about her asking for her privileged, well-supported child to receive additional attention. In Harvard University professor Sara Lawrence-Lightfoot's book on parent-teacher conferences, *The Essential Conversation*, she notes that "when parents plead with the teacher to be fair to their child, they are usually asking for special consideration for the youngster. They want the teacher to consider the unique struggles and strengths of the child and offer a differentiated response. But when teachers talk about being 'fair' to everyone, they mean giving equal amounts of attention, judging everyone by the same objective, universal standards, using explicit and public criteria for making judgments."[1] I understand what this woman wants, even as I'm determined not to give it to her.

Except that even as I remind myself of this, I feel myself sliding. "Look," I say. "Even though I know you're worried, I really think Kevin is going to be fine. And to a great degree, that's because he *has* been doing fine. Clearly, you're doing something right."

This is when the tears start. I reach for the tissues on my desk. "No need," Erica says with a smile, holding up some tissues. "I came prepared."

"I know this is hard," I continue. "This school can be an intimidating place. This department" — I wave my hand toward my colleagues just beyond my office door — "can be intimidating. I guess I can be intimidating."

"Yes," she says firmly, with a laugh that's somewhere between a poke and a jab.

This time I'm the one who nods with a grim smile. I remind her that I'm going to meet Kevin in a few hours. Mom can expect him to come home with a road map for how to revise the essay.

I don't have the impression that Erica considers this much of gesture, even a victory, even though I mean it to be. She stands, thanking me. Neither of us is feeling particularly satisfied. The customs of the moment call for professions of goodwill and closure, but we're going through the motions. I may feel like I've done a good job, but I know *she* doesn't feel that way. And something tells me that no matter what happens from here on out, she never will.

My meeting with Kevin is easier. Green-eyed, olive-skinned, and entering with the build of a smallish halfback, he seems self-contained, betraying little of the angst Erica reported that morning, though I realize that doesn't mean he hasn't been feeling it. We go over the essay and together hammer out an outline for revision. I go a little further than I usually do in these situations by typing it up and printing it out rather than relying on a notepad or having the student do it. I want Erica to have concrete evidence of the kind she craves. Kevin seems to accept all this as a matter of course. Like Erica, he's polite and thanks me before he leaves. But there's no real warmth the way there often is with kids for whom I do a good deal less.

The irony of all this is that whether or not Erica realizes it, or whether or not I really want to, I'm going to be giving this kid a little more attention for months to come. Consciously or unconsciously, I'll be more careful, if for no other reason than to deflect further complaints. Parents — and, especially, students — often worry that parental squawking will result in teachers treating students more severely. That may happen, but from where I sit such fears are usually exaggerated. More often than not, the technique works. Which is why well-educated and privileged parents are inclined to resort to it.

A few days later I get the revised version of the essay from Kevin, one for which he got additional input from the school's learning specialist. It's first-rate, successfully addressing the issues I raised and evincing a much tighter alignment between his thesis and the evidence he uses to support it. I take note of verbs like *opine*, which signals Erica's presence looming over Kevin's shoulder. Before grading it, I write Kevin and ask him, as per recent school policy, to acknowledge any kind of outside help he received. He writes back a missive consisting of three names: mine, the learning specialist, and Erica's. I write again asking him to elaborate a bit. He does, explaining that Mom's role was that of proofreader. I read the essay over again and decide that he missed an opportunity to use one of the readings (something I had pointed out to him earlier) and to acknowledge the counterargument for the one he's advancing. So I give him an A–. I might have given him the straight A if this was what had come to me the first time around, and if I had more confidence that it really was his work. Is that unfair? I decide no: making allowances cuts two ways. I think, not for the first time, how much I appreciate those kids who quietly go about the business of excellence (and those who quietly go about the business of not-such excellence) without this degree of intervention. In any event, Erica and Kevin have mastered the rules of the game and are playing it to their advantage.

And as annoyed as I am, I'm aware that the other extreme can be even more problematic. Disconnected parents sap the energy of a school in all kinds of ways, whether in terms of requiring staff to track them down when there's a problem, failing to support a child's work (not to mention turn in necessary paperwork when they need to), or failing to pitch in with the kind of energy that can lift the morale of students and teachers alike. There's a correlation between parent activism and class status, though in my experience there are certainly remote or uncooperative parents at every level of the pecking order.

On the same day I graded Kevin's essay, I received another subpar essay from another student, whom I directed to revise the piece without thinking much about it (this kid had actually failed the test on which Kevin scored 70 percent). When I read his revised essay, a few days after my meeting with Erica, it's still bad. I'm trying to figure out what grade to give it when I stop myself and decide that instead of putting a grade on it, I'm going to tell the kid we need to talk and work on it some more. He may be chagrined, afraid, or angry, but it's the right thing to do.

Take that, Erica.

HOME WORK

The phone on my desk is ringing when I arrive in my office at 8:17 on the Thursday morning in the week before winter break, though with the temperature stuck in the thirties, fall foliage is a distant memory. I pick up the receiver—how much longer are there going to be phones on desks?—while simultaneously trying to slip out of my coat. I'm tempted not to answer it.

"Hello?"

"Mr. Dewey?"

"Speaking."

"I'm so glad to have reached you. This is Ruth, Jason's mom? We met at the basketball game a couple weeks ago."

"Yes, of course. How are you?" In my mind I see nothing, no name, no face. But Jason—Jason Simkins—will be enough to work with. I drape my coat over my desk chair, pull my laptop out of my briefcase, and power it up.

"Well, I've been better," she's says. "I'm calling about the History Day project. As you know, Jason's working with Tom Schlacter."

"Yes." I sort of do know that. I've got a hard copy of the master list somewhere in my inbox. I begin to rustle through it.

"A thoroughly depressing subject, if you ask me." Now I remember: they're doing the decision to drop the atomic bomb. Originally they wanted to do World War II, but I told them the subject was too broad. They've narrowed it down to the bomb and are working on a PowerPoint (the first refuge of scoundrels). The first draft I saw was not too prom-

ising. Big slabs of text, relatively weak in conceptual organization. Technical glitches. Normally one or both of them
would be working with Joey Rizzo. But Joey has grand plans
for a tabletop reenactment of Pickett's Charge that he says
he's been working on with Roy Thomas. Ominously, I've seen
nothing new on Jason and Tom's project since they handed in
their notably sketchy first draft last week, only an e-mail with
a string of queries that could have been answered if they'd
actually studied the assignment.

Then I realize that I've not been paying close attention to
Ruth, who has been explaining the series of obstacles Jason
and Tom have encountered. "It doesn't help matters any that
Tom lives so far downtown. He never wants to come to our
place. Did you know that they spent *all night* working on this
Saturday?"

Given the taciturnity of both of these boys, I'm tempted to
ask how I *would* know that, but bite my tongue. I also imagine
an empty pizza box, a Madden NFL game on a laptop, and
vintage Ludacris blaring from some external speakers. Still, I
feel a twinge of unease. Truth is, the History Day Project has
long been a sore point among some administrators and colleagues, who think it asks too much of the kids at a difficult
time of year. We have revisited the subject from time to time
as a department and concluded that the pluses outweigh the
minuses. For grading purposes we like to have a substantial
gradewide assessment at the end of the quarter, and we see
bona fide value in a group undertaking in which students get
to choose their topic and work on it in a planned sequence of
stages. And some of the final results are truly extraordinary.
We routinely place finalists in the annual New York City History Day competition and often have a clutch of kids who go
on to the state level. Alas, that's not likely to be the case here.

"I'm sorry to hear that," I say soothingly about the all-nighter. "I know this is a difficult undertaking. That's why I always emphasize at the start of the project that students need to think carefully about with whom they're going to work and I repeatedly tell them that the quality of their collaboration is an important dimension of what this is all about. I also emphasize that they stand or fall together, and that if one kid coasts and another kid does all the work, that itself can be a valuable lesson."

"Well, I'm not sure I agree with you about that," she says. "Don't get me wrong—I'm not saying that Jason has handled this perfectly. He can be lazy. But I knew as soon as I heard that he was can be working with Tom that there were going to be problems. Tom is a nice kid, but I don't think he pulls his weight, intellectually or otherwise."

Not a kind assessment, but not an inaccurate one either. I click on my browser, go to my bookmarks, and choose the weather page. I see a graphic about an approaching storm.

"What I don't understand," she continues, "is the timing of this project. Why does it have to be just before the break? We're leaving for St. Bart's tomorrow morning. We've planned this trip for months, and I'm pulling the kids out of school tomorrow to get an early start."

I click on the WINTER WEATHER ADVISORY link. Snow to begin late this afternoon; six to ten inches by morning. Fine by me: I'm not going anywhere.

"Well," I respond, "the deadline for this project is something my department periodically reviews. But we've learned from experience that it makes more sense to have the project due before the break so that we clear the decks for kids to have a real vacation. Nobody likes to have a big assignment hanging over their heads going into a stretch of time off." Actually, I have traditionally had this assignment due a week *before* the break, but watching my own son scramble to complete it (a documentary about strategic bombing—the boys always seem to go for war) has led me to conclude that a little more time does make a difference. My son kept me out of the loop on that one, I'm happy to say. His partner's dad was a documentary filmmaker, so that was where they got most of their help.

Ruth is pressing the point: "I've got to tell you, an assignment like this really wreaks havoc on family life."

"Again, I'm sorry to hear that. Is there something you'd like me to do? Would you like me to talk with the boys?"

"That would be good," she says. "But what would really help is giving them more time. I don't think these two really understood what they've gotten themselves into. The geographic factor has really proven to be a major complication, and coming up with good times to collaborate has been a major, major problem. At my urging, they made plans to meet after school today—Tom is going to skip practice and come over—and my hope is that they'll forge a game plan to finish it. I think Jason will have lots of downtime between connecting flights and will be able to work while we're on the plane. They can communicate by e-mail or instant messaging or whatever. Do you think you could give them another day or two?"

I can't resist a smile. Normally I'd be in a position I really hate: having to say no. To accede to this request would not only precipitate an avalanche of similar ones—the word would be on the street almost immediately—but get me into trouble with my colleagues, as we've all sworn a blood oath to hold the line in the face of these pressures. I realize I'm taking a chance here, but if my bluff gets called, I can say I was certain, however mistakenly, that there was going to be a snow day.

"Well, I don't like to do this, but I understand there are extenuating factors in this particular situation. So I'll allow

Jason and Tom a little more time to finish this up. As long as I have it when we get back from break, there should be no harm done."

"I really appreciate that. I want you to know that Jason loves your class."

Yeah, right. "Thank you. I enjoy working with him."

"The best part of this," she tells me, adopting a confiding, even conspiratorial, tone, "is that Jason will be spending the second week of the break with his father. For once in his life, the man will actually have to pay attention to his son's needs. Can't wait to see *that.*"

"Glad to be of service," I say with a chuckle. And though I don't know why, I mean it. Though she's given me little reason to think so, I suspect her grievance with her ex, whoever he is, may well be legitimate. "Have a good trip, Ruth."

"Thank you, Mr. Dewey."

"Please call me Horace." But she's already hung up.

Turned out to be more like a foot of snow. But they got out in time. Jason came back with an enviable tan.

⁂

There are multiple frictions in the triangular relationship between parent, teacher, and student, ranging from grades to school budgets. But on a day-to-day basis, the most pervasive, if evanescent, is homework. It's a subject on which each party feels ambivalence. Students typically say they hate homework, but it's often the source of their most substantial achievements. Teachers feel they need homework to make class time more productive, but assigning it usually means more grading. Parents want to feel their children are learning, but they worry about the demands on their time and the way homework can sometimes interfere with extracurricular and family activities. (Having been involuntarily drawn into

my own children's projects, sometimes at the specific man-
date of teachers, I can sympathize with this exasperation.)

Of these three constituencies, it's teachers who are the
most stalwart champions of homework. Mastery of anything is always to some degree a matter of a willingness to
invest — and a willingness to waste — time in the pursuit
of long-term gain. This is a truth that students experience
in realms ranging from sports to computer games. Not all
students are eager to make such an investment in Spanish
or chemistry, though they might get why their parents and
teachers want that for them.

Which is not to say that homework is always assigned
thoughtfully or usefully by teachers. Inexperienced or lazy
ones will sometimes use homework as a crutch to compen-
sate for failures to use class time efficiently. Or they will assign homework that has no clear relationship to the material
being covered in class. Or assign it without assessing it in a
timely way — or at all, an omission that breeds resentment
and fosters corrosive corner-cutting by students. I have a real
problem with colleagues who take weeks or months to give
back essays. It's disrespectful of kids and counterproductive
when there's a deadening lag in getting meaningful feedback
on what they've done.

Even if one assumes that every teacher is thoughtful about
the way homework is deployed, taking up to a half-dozen
subjects at a time creates significant stress in even the best-
organized student's life. It's not unusual in some school
districts for students to routinely have over three hours of
homework a night, a particularly daunting prospect for a kid
in a play or on a team who returns from school on a late bus,
has dinner, and gets to work circa 7:30 p.m., twelve or more
hours after the day has begun. While schools often have cir-
cuit breakers of various kinds in place for this kind of prob-

lem (no homework over weekends or holiday breaks, makeup provisions for students saddled with multiple assessments on the same day, et al.), school schedules are such complicated organisms with so many moving parts that it's virtually impossible to craft an even work flow for any given kid. Even if this *were* possible from an academic standpoint, the discretionary choices students make — clubs, theater, sports — and their varying ability to juggle such balls complicate any attempt to create a truly level playing field. Under the circumstances, teachers can not only plausibly say they *can't* know what else their students are doing but also that they *shouldn't* allow such knowledge to become a consideration, lest their particular enterprise be crippled altogether.

It's for reasons like these that education reformers like Alfie Kohn argue for the elimination of homework entirely.[1] Such arguments get additional support when one considers how little a role it plays in leading educational powers like Finland. And how *much* of a role it plays in others like South Korea, where saddling students with extra work has become an arms race of sorts, generating so much misery and alarm that the government has resorted to police raids on tutoring classes that run beyond the state-mandated curfew of 10:00 p.m.[2]

Perhaps predictably, I will state that I'm a homework partisan. I try to be intelligent and efficient about it. Even more than with work undertaken during class time, students should have a clear understanding of how what they're being asked to do fits into a larger curricular schema or prepares them for an upcoming assessment. Homework should be relatively modest in scope — the rule at my school is an average of forty-five minutes per subject per night, though that can add up if you've got a bunch of classes — and ideally give students some leeway in when they complete it, as in an assignment given on Monday but not due until later in the week.

There are two core tasks that homework is good for—that homework is *uniquely* good for. These tasks are alike in that they demand a measure of concentration and reflection difficult to come by during the school day. The process of education is inherently social; while homeschooling has its devotees and may be necessary for any number of reasons, children learn best in school because interacting with peers on multiple levels is central to learning (including the acquisition of self-knowledge through comparison with others). And yet—in part for that very reason—an educational process that does not build in opportunities for solitude and absorbing lessons, implicit as well as explicit ones, is incomplete. Students need time to *make sense* of things. This work of making sense can happen in the hurly-burly of class discussion or in scribbling down notes while a teacher talks, but processing and integrating information is typically work that gets completed off site.

The first important homework task is reading. Adults typically laud it, for themselves and children—"Readers are leaders," a beloved uncle of mine, a construction worker who as far as I can tell was indifferently educated at best, used to say—but few of us really have much stamina for it. Reading requires a focus that's difficult to sustain because there's so little time in the day, or because of our physiological limitations, or both. I think of reading as akin to physical exercise: the more you do it, the better you get at it and the faster your mind works. Reading may well be less important for the actual content you encounter than for the habits of mind it inculcates—attentiveness, imagination, a capacity for abstraction. In the end, reading is the sine qua non of learning: everything else is a shortcut, a compensation, a substitution (like a fad diet in lieu of exercise). To use a culinary metaphor:

reading is home cooked; getting it in lecture form is store-bought. Sure, reading takes longer. But it's just plain better.

Precisely because reading is so difficult, teachers should assign it with care—something which, alas, is difficult when one is subject to districtwide mandates. Textbooks are like baby food: they're age appropriate, relatively substantial, and segmented into measured servings. But that doesn't mean they're tasty. Far better are selections chosen by a well-read teacher with a sharp eye for the relevant newspaper article, blog post, short story, or poem. As in so many other realms, less is more. In part that's because for students and teacher to read together, to *close*-read sentences and passages, is an excellent use of class time after students come to class having already had a first taste of a piece of text. Reading *intensively*, which is to say reading things more than once, is among the most important wellsprings of learning.

Reading is so crucial because it's foundational for success in an even more demanding intellectual task that's also best undertaken as homework: writing. Writing is among the most complex neurological tasks the human brain performs, and it's hard work. Paradoxically, good writing seems effortless. Which is one of the reasons students find it so daunting: it *seems* like it should be easy, and when it isn't they assume they're bad at it, which makes them even less willing to undertake it. But knowing that it's hard for everyone will only get you so far. Writing is like bench-pressing a lot of weight—you have to work yourself up to it. That's what school is for: creating a space where such activities are promoted and sustained, precisely because there's really nowhere else it would happen in such a concentrated way and on a mass scale.

I don't think you want a primer on writing from me at this point; there are plenty of them out there. For now I'll simply observe that there's a lot a good teacher can do to improve student writing, and much of it should take place in the classroom. This includes information delivery, ranging from a definition of a thesis — I like a "not-obvious but true assertion"[3] — to an explanation of how to cite a source. It also includes workshop sessions where students discuss each other's work. Structuring such encounters is what good teachers do.

But — really — the single most important reason to ask students to write is that it's something that they must do alone. Only when they're by themselves, grappling, seeking, struggling to communicate with somebody else, are they fully engaged in the task of learning. Actually, they can't really begin to explain something to someone else until they've explained it to themselves, which is what first drafts are for. Writing is also a collaborative enterprise, in that peers and parents can provide feedback, and in some cases teachers can sit beside students and coach them through the process. But even when this happens, there still needs to be a time and place where students follow through on their own. The coach must step aside.

The coaching analogy is a very rich one for understanding teaching generally, but it has particular value in the context of homework. Coaches prescribe workouts, some of which are executed on the field of play but much of many of which take place off site. The coach can't monitor any given athlete continuously, nor can a coach be certain that a particular routine will pay off equally or at all for every athlete. It's a game of percentages that, should the student honor the coach's instructions, is likely to yield long-term gain. Beyond some general parameters (like the length of a practice and care for the health of the athletes), the coach doesn't know or care what else the players may have to do, and a coach's personal regard for a player should not cloud the coach's judgment about who is or isn't in shape. There are no guarantees. But the best way to win games is to practice.

※◎※

The goals of the History Day project that Jason and Tom are working on are a bit different from what I've been outlining here. My school participates in National History Day, a program that annually involves fifty thousand students from forty-nine states who work within the parameters of an annually chosen theme like "Turning Points in History," "Revolution, Reaction and Reform," or "Rights and Responsibilities."[4] Students can work alone or collaborate in groups of up to three people, and can choose formats from a menu of options that include tabletop exhibitions, documentaries, dramatic presentations, and websites. My colleagues and I believe that the work of formulating arguments may be easier for students when working in media other than traditional essays, which is why this project is a capstone assessment for the fall semester (a gradewide research essay is the main undertaking for the spring).

We're pretty upfront with students when we assign this project in early November that it's as much about managing the enterprise as it is the content. That means planning ahead for deadlines that come up in stages: topic, bibliography, first draft, final draft. We tell them: choose your partners carefully, because you sink or swim together. Someone who does all the work will get the same grade as a member of your team that does none. (In fact, we keep an eye on this and make mental notes to balance the ledgers in some silent way.) "I'm not sure I agree with you about that," Ruth had said when I explained my colleagues' thinking in our phone conversation, and she may be right. But this is how we play this particular game, and revealing her son's difficulty in playing it is part of the point.

For all our planning and justifications, however, we never entirely feel we're in control of the assignments we give. Loopholes and ambiguities inevitably present themselves; so do unplanned exigencies like snowstorms. My delight in conferring upon Ruth and Jason Thompson an extension dissipates quickly as my colleagues in the history department realize the storm is creating a logistical mess, and a flurry of e-mails swirls among us. If the History Day project were a run-of-the-mill essay, we might simply expect students to e-mail their work to us, whether or not school was in session. But given the number of projects that actually have to be brought in and set up (the kindly librarians have given us some space), we can't expect that. Since we need to be uniform, we decide the project will have to be due the first day back after the break. The very thing we were trying to prevent—having kids with homework over the holidays—has come to pass.

Jason and Tom's project, long on images and short on interpretation, gets a B. On the acknowledgments panel of their PowerPoint, Jason thanks his dad "for help in proofreading, and for the pizza."

In the aftermath of the year's assignment, we decide that maybe a postbreak due date isn't such a bad idea after all. In fact, we agree, the thing to do is to have draft workshops the first week back and have the projects due the second week. That will create a grading squeeze before the semester ends, but it seems worth it. For teachers no less than students, there's no substitute for experience. We learn by doing—and redoing.

AMONG COLLEAGUES

SMART BOARD, DUMB TEACHER

Midmorning, early February. Outside, it's frigid. Inside, the radiator heat makes me woozy. A few history teachers have gathered here in my classroom, at the behest of principal Hannah Osborne, for training on the new Smart Boards we've all received as part of the school's latest technology upgrade. One more round of being prodded to learn about things we never want to know and will be incompetent with when we try. I've made my peace with Smart Boards as a matter of using them as glorified projectors. But now we're being nudged to use them for classroom note taking and other tasks. So it is that the rising waters of technological innovation still manage to reach us. Now *we* get to be the confused, bored, and resentful students.

Our technology maven, Jessica, an impressively competent outside consultant who's clearly younger than her salt-and-pepper mane would suggest, is chatting away about all the tools and applications that are now at our disposal with the new software that can be easily downloaded at . . . I didn't quite hear and don't want to ask. My colleague Tony Snowden, who's always been an early adopter — he had an iPhone on day one — is querying her closely on how to access the feature she had been showing us before she moved on to whatever it is that she's now doing. "You just go and adjust the settings on the system preferences menu," she says, and Tony nods with satisfaction. "Just be sure you have it on the default settings option," she adds.

"*Oh,*" Bob Oros says sarcastically. "The *system preferences* menu. Naturally."

"Of course," Tony says in a tone of good-natured ribbing, "your default setting is permanently set to off, Bob."

"Absolutely," he replies, happy to be the butt of a joke.

Our maven renders a thin smile. I have a fleeting sense of sympathy for her: it must be tedious to talk to idiots all day. I glance up at the clock. I'm missing a workout on the Stairmaster; the gym is usually empty this period.

Actually, there had been a point when I was looking forward to this session. I came back from the winter break to find my old Smart Board gone, which didn't matter all that much because I always continued to use my old blackboard (though I'm always scrounging around for chalk, which invariably runs across the back of my pants when I turn and face the class). At last year's professional day, I had watched in amazement as one of my colleagues in the science department wrote with a virtual marker on a whiteboard and then instantly turned the words into type. Given the complaints and queries I constantly get whenever I write on the blackboard, this was something I was truly interested in learning about. Despite a twinge of unease to see those slate boards go — I was surprised when picking up my daughter from a recent playdate to see that her host had a huge blackboard in his kitchen, surely a sign that what was once a commonplace object was well on its way to becoming a cool artifact — I was ready to finish stepping into the twenty-first century. Though of course many of the skills I was most eager to learn were ones I could have picked up years ago.

Our maven is just now beginning to demonstrate the latest aspects of the handwriting-to-text feature, and I raise my hand. "Could we use a real-life example?" I ask. She's reluctant, I can see from the fleeting expression of irritation that almost imperceptibly crosses her face. But I leap to the front of the room, grab a green virtual marker, and start writing some points I plan to use in class that very day. "You might want to go a little slower," she says from behind me, having adjusted to my imposition. I write:

SOURCES OF WEALTH IN THE POST–CIVIL WAR WEST
- Land (farming)
- Mining
- Ranching

It quickly becomes apparent, however, that my handwriting on the Smart Board is even worse than it is on a blackboard—smears of green mush.

"You have to learn to write differently," our maven says.

"Is that all?" Bob asks.

She ignores him. "You have to write more with your shoulder." She demonstrates the motion. I nod as if I understand and grab the virtual eraser, dismayed that my sludge doesn't disappear.

"You have to put the marker down first before you can erase."

I do so. Now the eraser works, more or less. When I put it down, she comes over, takes the red marker, and models how I should actually write. It of course looks perfectly legible.

"Now," she explains as I take my seat again, "in order to turn this into type you must first turn it into an object." She moves her index finger across her text, and a box forms. She moves her finger to a small square on the upper right-hand corner of the box, and a string of suggested words appears: "Sources of welts / Sources of welfare / Sources of wealth" and a few more I can't quite take in. She selects "Sources of wealth" and voilà: handwriting becomes type.

"Now you turned 'sources of wealth' into what you call an object," I observe. "But do you have to make a separate object for each line on the Smart Board?"

"Probably."

Probably? Now I'm truly discouraged. It all seems like so much work: making sure you have the right settings; making sure you don't pick up the eraser while you still have a marker; making sure you write the right way; drawing boxes around the objects; hoping you'll get the right option for turning it into text. Surely it's simpler just to pick up a piece of chalk, no?

"I gotta run," says Tony. This session has been pitched too low for him. "Good luck," he says as he exits, winking to the maven, who smiles in appreciation for his gesture. I look up at the clock again and see that if I leave now I can squeeze in that workout after all. I see Bob is also motioning to go. He's saying something to the maven that makes her break into a broad smile: a divide has been bridged. But not a technological divide — he and I have learned little useful information. We probably needed a day, not an hour. But a day would just be too much with everything else we have going on.

That night as I brush my teeth, it occurs to me that some of my students must feel the way I did earlier that day — probably not about technology, which they seem to take to instinctively, but about some of the academic work they're asked to do. They find it hard but pretend they don't or try to laugh it off. They fake their way for a while, maybe get the hang of some aspects of a subject, and try to keep moving. It's the skill of improvising that ends up getting developed — the bluffing, faking, and ad hoc adaptation.

Three days later, a canceled meeting unexpectedly gives me a half-hour, and I walk into my empty classroom. I turn on the computer and Smart Board and begin stumbling around. A half-hour later, I've managed to write "Tomorrow's class will meet in the library" and turn it into text. A triumph. I have no clear idea how facile I'll ever be on this thing; I suspect I'll settle into some simple routines that I won't wander from very much. But I know I have to do this. There's some part of me that will die less quickly if I do. Truth be told, I'm a little surprised, and more than a little pleased, that I'm not quite ready to be erased.

POSITIONS

The e-mail I get is mild-mannered—that's just Erin McDonald's way—but with an unmistakable subtext of frustration. "I realize you've got a lot of balls in the air, Horace," she writes, "and one of the last things you're probably thinking about is room placements for next year." (She's right: it's months away.) "And while I know these things are complicated, I'd like to make a request that if possible, you don't slot me into Room H267. Thanks so much."

Erin's is one of thirteen e-mails I get that morning, some of which require my immediate attention. I might have forgotten about it altogether if I didn't see her working at her desk alongside a few colleagues as I leave my office to head to the copying machine. "So what's the deal with H267?" I ask her.

She sighs. "Well, for one thing, it's the computer in there," she explains. "Angela insists that we use her PC, but I'm a Mac person. Which isn't that big a deal, but Angela gets touchy whenever we change the settings. And actually it's an old PC, and it always seems like the Smart Board connections don't work, which means I have to get tech in there, and of course I can't half the time. My ninth graders can barely sit still in the first place, and having to fiddle with the controls makes it hard for me to keep control of the classroom."

I nod. Room H267 is "Angela's room," by which I mean it's the unofficial property of one of my senior colleagues, where all her classes meet and where she stores her books. Posters and postcards from Asia cover the walls—she teaches Chinese history and has been there various times—and travel photos are on the desk where the computer in question sits. Having such a space is one of the perks of seniority at my school, one that has become problematic in recent years as space has gotten tighter and junior colleagues like Erin — who, truth be told, is not really so junior anymore — often shuttle between a series of classrooms to teach their classes.

Still, I'm a little surprised that she's making an issue of this. I'm even more surprised when her colleagues enter into the fray with unsolicited comments. "I have to say, Horace, Erin has a point," Ed Vinateri says. He's got his eye on H111, which just might become his if our colleague Frank Dileo retires as expected. "It's one thing to have all your classes in one place and to put up your own decorations. But when the computer really gets in the way of instruction, we're talking about a different thing. I had a hell of time in there last year. It's really old; I don't understand why it hasn't been replaced."

Susanna Alvarez is shaking her head. "I *hate* that computer," she says. "I thought it was just me. I had to cancel an in-class essay assignment last week because I couldn't get a video going that I wanted to use to set it up. I'm kinda glad to learn that I'm not a total idiot."

"And Erin's right," Ed continues. "Angela can be touchy. I asked her awhile back if we could change the setup. She said it would be really inconvenient for her to keep changing back and forth. And she sounded really aggrieved that I would even ask."

Ugh. I seem to have walked right into a mess. It's clear Erin, Ed, and Susanna want me to do something about this. A dreaded conversation with Angela looms. Why, oh why, did I ever agree to become department chair?

The answer, of course, is that Angela talked me into it.

❧❦❧

In terms of professional hierarchy, teaching is a relatively flat occupation. For the most part, a teacher is a teacher—there are no tiers the way there is in academe, with its ranks of assistant, associate, and full professor (with the endowed chair as Valhalla). Some schools have assistant teachers, but they're usually the literal or figurative equivalent of graduate students, apprentices on their way to bona fide teacher status. There are also teacher assistants, members of a different occupation without instruction responsibilities, who do things like patrol lunchrooms and supervise outdoor activities. Certainly veteran teachers are recognized, principally in terms of their paychecks. But if you're looking for a significant increase in salary, status, and responsibility, you pretty much have to go into administration. In this regard, teachers are a bit like reporters, for whom professional advancement is usually a matter of advancing to an editing position.

The problem for teachers and reporters is that they're often reluctant to relinquish positions that are as much a matter of love as of money. Indeed, it's not unusual for journalism executives and high school principals to keep plying their old trade even as they devote most of their time to their managerial responsibilities—or to surrender the latter entirely as they near retirement and return to the rank and file. The compensation structure of these professions reflects these realities: financial officers often exert pressure to hire young people for entry-level jobs because they're cheaper, and to tamp down the rate of salary adjustment, even impose a ceiling, as veterans reach late middle age.

Meanwhile, the core labors of the job don't change. Teachers get better with experience, which often means achieving greater efficiencies in managing their time. But one year can run into the next with disconcerting seamlessness. (As I've indicated, perhaps the biggest exception comes with the introduction of new technologies, which can be disruptive—a term with none of the positive connotations of which the entrepreneurial classes are so fond.) Insofar as there are rewards for longevity, they're often in the form of creature comforts — parking spaces, priority on new equipment, favorable scheduling, and, of course, classrooms.

One important exception to the regime I'm describing is the role of department chair in middle and high schools. It's a hybrid position, involving mostly teaching with a fraction of administrative work thrown in, typically in the form of managing a small budget for things like supplies, making staffing decisions, and setting or maintaining matters of policy among a subset of people that's smaller than a school or grade. The way people are appointed to this position, and its relative status, varies widely. Sometimes it's considered a thankless job that's difficult to fill; in other places it's a post for which competition is intense; in still others the appointment is made by consensus. There's also variation in the length of one's tenure in the job, which can rotate within a department after a fixed number of years or be held by an individual indefinitely.

From what I understand, the position of chair at my school was not all that desirable in the years before I arrived. The post conferred a 5 percent increase in salary for the person who held it, with a 25 percent release of one's teaching load. Perhaps because finding people willing to serve was proving difficult, the administration sweetened the pot by making the salary raise 10 percent. That seemed to do the trick. The chair does not rotate (though this is emerging as best practice, and there's some talk of changing our practice), and I have one colleague who's been in the post for over a decade. For the most part, however, there seems to have been reasonably steady turnover stemming from retirements and promotion to administrative positions.

I was hired at East Hudson to replace someone who had been a longtime department chair. I took over this man's teaching slot; the chair passed, by consensus, to a colleague who performed the job estimably. When, two years ago, she left to take a position at another school, we again had to decide who the chair would be. The most senior figure in the department, Bob Oros, had no interest. Next in line was Angela, but she had just been awarded a sabbatical, which she planned to spend in Japan. She was also interested in the prospect of a PK–12 curriculum coordinator position that was reportedly to open up the following year.

"You should take the chair," she told me at the time. "You're the logical choice. Ed would come forward if you didn't, and he would probably be fine. But I think the administration would probably be more comfortable with you, and if you say you want the job no one is likely to contest you for it." She said this in such a way that led me to conclude she'd been working behind the scenes. Angela and I had always been friendly: around the same age, with daughters the same age (there had been occasional playdates, but none lately). We shared an outlook rooted in our similar places in the life cycle, and though we socialized outside school settings only rarely, I always enjoyed it when we did so.

"*You're* really the logical choice," I countered. "And I'm not sure I'm really cut out for it." I meant this. I'd never managed people in my life and had come to see myself as a relatively free agent, someone who wasn't bossed around but didn't boss anyone else around either. My role model in this regard was Bob, who guarded his independence jealously—in large measure by being beyond reproach as an educator par excellence.

"You'll be fine," Angela said. "Better than you know."

The thought of running for department chair had crossed

my mind before my conversation with Angela, but it was the conversation with her that led me to take it seriously. Four things ultimately swayed me. The first was a conversation with Ed, who joined me for lunch at one point to gauge my interest, clearly angling for the chair himself. I began to see, more clearly than I had, that I did not want to be his subordinate, less because I had any objection to him than because I didn't like the idea of a boss younger than myself when I was in a position to do something about it. The second was the small office that went with the job — I had long coveted some quieter space than the open room I'd been sharing with four other colleagues. Third was the money: the 10 percent boost in salary would translate to a car payment, and my family needed a new minivan. Finally — and this was important — I would be taking over a department of competent people with a high degree of amity. I thought that even a conflict-averse person like me could handle it. Or should *make* himself handle it.

I put my name forward, was chosen by a process that seemed mysterious — Hannah Osborne did some kind of informal polling — and was announced as the new chair. The position was daunting in some ways because there was a host of routine annual tasks I had to master, though I got plenty of help. I made a couple mistakes arising from overzealous devil's advocacy in department meetings and in mediating conflicts with parents, but was pulled aside by colleagues, among them Angela, who gently suggested that I tack back to a more supportive stance. This was hard — I had a couple of anxious days and considered the possibility that I lacked the touch for the job. But I tried to learn from my mistakes (making it a point to praise people more often) and gradually began to feel I was settling into the role.

Angela did not fare quite as well. She had a great trip, but the curriculum coordinator position was put on hold pend-

ing an administrative overhaul, and in the meantime she irritated our head of school, Alan Sanders, for criticizing his
handling of a tenure case. She was said to be on the job market, but nothing had come up. Fortunately, her teaching slot
was still there, and she quietly resumed her duties. Perhaps
if I were a nicer guy I would have stepped aside and let her
take the chair position, assuming that could be easily done.
But I was growing attached to the job (and definitely attached
to those car payments). I tried to pay Angela deference when
it came to things like the electives she wanted to teach and
when her classes could be held. I figured that was to be my
role here.

Until I got Erin's e-mail about that damned computer.

⁂

Over the course of the next day, I solicit the opinions of a few
more people. Another colleague not present in the room that
day affirms the views of Ed, Erin, and Susanna. A colleague
from the English department who uses H267 a couple of days
a week feels less strongly but would certainly like to see a new
computer setup. A guy from the tech crew explains that were
it not for Angela's request to do otherwise, he would have
replaced the old PC years ago — and is irked by the stream of
requests he gets to fix glitches. He says there's money in the
technology budget for a new-generation Smart Board.

I dread confronting Angela, partly because I don't like
awkward conversations generally and partly because I suspect she's feeling a bit tender after her professional setbacks.
Hoping to pass the buck, I describe the situation to the principal, Hannah Osborne, and ask her advice. I'm pleased that
that Hannah — who daily handles such social frictions deft-
ly — offers to talk to Angela instead. *Phew.*

But this doesn't seem quite right. This is largely a departmental matter and probably should be resolved within departmental channels. Not doing so would make me look weak and might well make Angela feel worse. I compromise: a note by e-mail.

> Hi Angela,
> Hope you had a good weekend. Angela, a number of our colleagues have expressed concerns about the computer set-up in H267. I wonder how you would feel if we got a Smart Board in there instead of the old set-up. Let me know what you think. Thanks.

Minutes later, Angela responds:

> Horace,
> Thanks for the note. Is this about Ed? As you know, I've used that room for years without a problem. I hope that you're not thinking of dismantling a system that has worked well for years. It would set an unfortunate precedent.

I write back:

> Actually, Angela, a number of people have raised objections. If you like, I can list them and you can try to work out arrangements with them individually [something I hope she won't take me up on]. I'm not challenging your claim on this room as a matter of holding your classes in there or the posters, photos, etc. But as you know, space has been at a premium lately, and you share H267 with a number of teachers, past and present. I feel their wishes have to be taken into account. We can also submit this for Hannah to resolve, if you like.

Her first response came instantly. But now I hear nothing for the rest of the day. Thankfully, I don't see Angela. But what's happening? Is she talking to lots of people? Is she mobilizing opinion against my meddling? I think I've considered all the angles here, but I'm still rattled. It's on my mind when I wake up at 3:00 a.m., circling as I struggle to get back to sleep. I'm also mad at myself for allowing such a trivial matter to take up so much psychic space. If something like this is giving me trouble, how the hell am I going to handle a *real* problem?

When I awaken at 6:30 an e-mail, sent minutes earlier, is waiting for me. Maybe Angela hasn't gotten much sleep either.

> Horace,
> We'll get the Smart Board. I trust this will satisfy any disgruntled individuals and let us get back to work.
> Thanks.

Victory. But it feels icky. How many months until that van gets paid off?

I decide as I get dressed that we won't make any moves until the end of the semester. When I run into Angela in the faculty lounge later that morning I tell her I'm sorry about this, thank her for her flexibility, and explain that we'll wait until current electives are over. She nods, not making eye contact but looking more sad than angry. In the days that follow, I don't feel any particular animus coming from her, but she doesn't engage me in conversation as she usually does either. When I walk by H267, I notice a new, freshly unboxed computer.

I don't really think this will be the end of the matter. It may well lurk for years, a grievance that will pop up above the surface when the next conflict erupts. Maybe Angela will exact revenge on Erin or Susanna in some form I'll never know about. Or she'll get to be the populist in mobilizing against some departmental policy that I'll feel obliged to defend. As faculty politics goes, this is pretty tame stuff. But you never entirely escape it.

One thing's for sure: I'll never manage anything larger than a history department. I'm just not that good at it. I'll stick to discussions about Benjamin Franklin and the clever ways other people have solved their problems.

AMONG ADMINISTRATORS

COMPLAINTS

❦❧❦

"He's such goddamned evil little troll." Rick Engels reaches for his Guinness. It's 4:50 on Friday afternoon in September, and the regulars have gathered at our watering hole a few blocks off campus.

"Well, now, that's a little harsh," Denise Richardson says.

Rick puts down his glass. "Fine. Jesus loves him. I'll limit myself to 'evil little troll.'" Alice Alessandra smiles at this; Troy Ricci laughs. Ed Vinateri nods.

"You're just saying that because he didn't give you that extra line in your department," Denise says.

"And because Elsa didn't get tenure," Eddie adds.

"And because he wears that ridiculous hat!" Alice shouts. Clearly she's had a couple; her drink has a pink hue that I don't recognize.

"Oh my God," Gerri Thomas adds, shaking her head. "That hat."

"That enough reason not to like him?" Rick asks Denise.

"You're just mad because you wish you could look half as good in in a hat like that," she replies. Everyone breaks up into riotous laughter. Rick is a fashion-conscious gay man, and the boater in question—while hardly ridiculous from my admittedly pedestrian point of view—is eons away from his sensibility of skinny jeans, pointy boots, and cashmere scarves.

"Seriously," Rick says, when the laughter subsides, "the man has done a bunch of things I don't like. And that's OK—if I expected every head of school to comport himself to my standards, I think I would have gone insane twenty years—"

203

"Wait a second," Ed interrupts. "You're not implying that you're sane, are you, Rick?"

"Fuck you, Eddie," Rick says, planting a kiss on his cheek amid much laughter. But he's more focused on the point at hand. "People make decisions I disagree with all the time. But if there's one thing I can't *stand*, it's hypocrisy. So for him to get up there at that faculty meeting and ask all of us to give him the benefit of the doubt just *staggers* my imagination." He goes for another pull on his beer.

"Well, what do you expect him to say?" Denise asks. "He's embattled. He feels he's viewed with suspicion and distrust no matter what he does."

"Well, whose fault is that?" Ed asks. "Does he think we're just going to forget about what happened to Danny? He fires a teacher for a single remark taken out of context and we're supposed to give *him* the benefit of the doubt?"

"You know, Denise, if I didn't know better I'd say you're in the guy's pocket," Rick says.

"But you *do* know better, Rick."

Rick nods, backing off. "I do," he says. "Right, Horace?"

"Right." I take a swig of my own beer. Then I wait for what I hope is a decent interval to make a beeline for the bathroom so I can wipe off the smile pasted on my face.

❧

No school wants perpetual and pervasive conflicts between teachers and administrators. But if there was ever a God of Schooling, such a deity would surely ordain such tensions as a matter of checks and balances, a healthy ecosystem, or whatever other metaphor you might choose. Though—or because—teachers value their autonomy so highly, it's essential that there be people to monitor their behavior and try to maintain some measure of institutional consistency.

Conversely, the administrative tendency to centralize control is best tempered by a diffusion of power among teachers who follow rules with at least a modicum of interpretive flexibility. It's also inevitable, and good, that teachers will be constantly making ground-level decisions in dealing with unanticipated situations and responding to students whose histories and temperaments can't be codified. Yet teachers will sometimes need the advice and institutional authority that administrators provide. And teachers will make mistakes that require the talents and tact of administrators. So there's a real symbiosis there, as well as structural frictions.

The *degree* of symbiosis and the *intensity* of the structural friction vary widely from school to school, and sometimes within a school over time. Like sports teams, schools seem to have more and less successful climates for reasons that are not always clear. To be sure, financial challenges and demographic pressures are certain to inflame tensions, as well as cause them. But I've seen seemingly prosperous places that are rife with conflict, as well as resource-challenged schools that have a real spirit of teamwork. Good leadership — which generally arises from people who know, like, and trust teachers — is often a magnet for talent, though principals are no more capable of working miracles than teachers are in environments where other elements (like material resources or engaged students/parents) are lacking.

Which is not to say that success equates to popularity. Effective administrators master the art of saying no. They also have to master the art of calibrated anger at teachers who neglect their obligations to their students or colleagues. Sometimes no one is more eager for administrators to play that role than other teachers, who appreciate the presence of someone willing to do police work they're reluctant to take on themselves. The desire to be liked may well be a universal impulse, and it's one that teachers in particular tend to exhibit (indeed, it's probably a big part of what impels them to the job, and what makes many of the good ones successful). But while administrators may well share this desire—and may act on it, with positive consequences for themselves and others—few people are likely to lose respect more quickly than administrators whose desire for approval is too obvious.

A further complicating factor in the teacher-administrator dynamic might be termed an imperative for tribalism. In more ways than one, teachers and administrators tend to stick to their kind. In part that's because they have distinctive worldviews; teachers tend to see their school in terms of classes and students, while administrators tend to think in bigger, system-based ways. Since both camps often find themselves challenged on the manner in which they do their jobs, they typically fraternize with their peers, a desire for support that ultimately reinforces (and very often intensifies) their feelings. Though they will tend toward civility in official settings, very often masking their hostility, they relish the chance to vent their feelings when they feel it's safe to do so—that is, when they're among their own tribe. Like at the bar on Friday afternoons.

Which is not to say that these tendencies are uniform or mindless. Very often members of one constituency will feel sympathy for the other, whether because of sharing a position on a specific issue or because of having common adversaries (like fiscally tight school boards). In fact, both teachers and administrators often demonstrate flexibility in their views, if not for the same reasons. For teachers, cultivating an appreciation for multiple perspectives is central to the educational enterprise pedagogically. For administrators, such an approach is indispensable for juggling multiple personalities and constituencies.

Such moments can seem more like the exception than the rule, however. It's generally more comfortable to take refuge in consensus opinion. This was certainly the case when it came to my view of Alan Sanders, who prompted such boisterous commentary at the bar that day.

A little background: Alan had arrived at the school a year and a half earlier, the first African American to ever hold the post. He had been the superintendent of a large school district approximately one hundred miles away, and generally it was his public school background more than his race that elicited comment. The previous head of the school had been of fourteen years' standing, and while no one questioned her competency and dedication, there had been growing discontentment—perhaps inevitable—with her attention to fundraising, which led some of my colleagues to assert that she was neglecting the day-to-day operations of the institution (in part because she didn't clearly delegate that job to a lieutenant). A series of pent-up hopes, ranging from major structural changes to new permutations in the pecking order, gave Alan's appointment an air of expectation oscillating between hope and anxiety.

As it turned out, his tenure got off to a highly controversial start. Three weeks into the school year, a physical education teacher named Danny Miller got into an argument with a recalcitrant student who was refusing to change into his gym clothes for class, claiming an undocumented injury. Danny and this student apparently knew each other relatively well—Danny had taught two siblings of the student, recently graduated—and was aware that he was gay, as were his classmates. In a moment of tense jocularity, Danny told the student to get his "faggoty ass into that locker room," and the student complied without further argument. Nor did he actually complain. It was other boys who reported the incident to their parents, and it was some of them who protested to the school administration, arguing that Danny was creating a hostile environment by using hate speech. The fact that the fifty-three-year-old Danny himself had recently served as the best man at his gay brother's wedding became widely known; this mattered to some and not to others. The student made a public statement of support for Danny, which condemned what he said but expressed the hope that no disciplinary action would be taken. Some said this testimonial was the single most important fact; others wondered whether it was the result of some kind of pressure (the language of the student's statement was a bit stilted). Still others said the real problem with what Danny said was its chilling effect and poor example for other students in his charge.

In at least one sense, however, these arguments were beside the point. Less than forty-eight hours after the parental protest was lodged, Danny Miller was fired. "[In] an institution fiercely committed to community integrity and student safety, there are some lines that must be drawn whatever the perceived mitigating circumstances," Alan asserted in the e-mail he sent out announcing the decision, his sole public comment on the matter. "We must strive to do what we think is right, even when the right action is also a painful action." Danny, who had apologized for his "stupid" remark, sued the school for wrongful termination, and as all relevant sides in the dispute were lawyered up, none would comment any further. Eight months later the case was settled out of court with both sides sworn to silence. The word on the street was that Danny received a low six figures in damages.

Alan's handling of the case became a referendum on his infant tenure. A small but quietly assertive minority, mostly parents, believed he had done the right thing, pointing out that this was not the first time Danny's tart tongue had gotten him into trouble. (He once called the head of school "bitchy" in the presence of other teachers after a faculty meeting where she was not present — he apologized after a female gym teacher called him out on that; there were also anecdotal reports of profanity on various playing fields over the years, a charge most people shrugged off.) Though of course the matter was never put to a vote, it was my impression that the majority of the faculty was dismayed by Alan's decision, principally because they considered it far too hasty: there were plenty of steps short of termination that would have sent a decisive message. Danny was a nineteen-year veteran of the school and generally well liked. The chair of the Faculty Council, an avowed feminist who had criticized him at the time of his "bitchy" comment, prepared a petition protesting the lack of due process in his case. All members of the PE department signed it. Student protests and school newspaper articles emphasized the free speech angle. There was also a strong there-but-for-the-grace-of-God factor for the not inconsiderable number of older white guys, like me, who viewed the whole affair more in sorrow than in anger.

And then there was Rick Engels. Rick was certainly not alone in expressing anger at Alan's decision — "does he think the word *nigger* has a single connotation?' he asked at one point, comparing it to the multivalent connotations of *faggot* — but no one was as vocal as he was. I knew of two lesbian members of the faculty; one, a member of Danny's department, had signed the petition; the other, an English teacher, had not, but had not volunteered an opinion openly as far as I knew. Faculty of color tended to side with Alan ("the word *nigger* pretty much *does* have one connotation when it's uttered by someone who would never be called one," a Spanish teacher, Ciara Gutierrez, told me). One exception was the chair of the foreign language department, Alberto Mores, a good friend of Rick's, who I'd heard describe Alan as a "dick."

I found myself wondering if there wasn't something flamboyant in the intensity of Rick's feelings about Alan, as if he believed his sexuality inoculated him from any suggestion of racial animus, since he was a member of a historically marginalized population. For all I knew, Rick was of color himself, though he certainly didn't look it. I also wondered if his expressions of support for Danny were more a statement about the capaciousness of his own tolerance than one of solidarity with a colleague. As far as I could tell, Rick had never been particularly close to Danny; they never sat together at faculty meetings or in the cafeteria, for example. Was that a valid observation? At some level I also recognized that my focus on these questions reflected some vulnerabilities in my own outlook. I always liked Rick—

—Well, no. The truth is I've never really liked Rick, something I've resisted admitting to myself, in part because he's a member of my department and we're generally reputed to be a congenial bunch. Does my reluctance to admit my distaste for him reflect homophobia? I've always disliked that term, as if one's objection to something like gay marriage was not about ideology or values but fear (which always seemed condescending—an opponent must not simply be resisted but diminished). Actually, I've never been opposed to gay marriage, though I'm old enough to be amused that so many gay people now apparently *want* to be married, since gay liberation at least initially seemed to be a matter of rejecting repressive middle-class norms. But as someone born before Stonewall, I know I have lingering biases about homosexuality, even if I have trouble seeing or admitting them.

In any event, this unease was only one source of my difficulty with the whole Danny Miller affair. The most glaring aspect was the way Rick's certitude about Alan highlighted my own ambivalence. I had in fact signed the petition on Danny's behalf. In part, that was because I did think Alan had been too hasty. But it was also because I did not want to be estranged from the colleagues I cared about most. Still, I can't say I was all that sorry to see Danny go; while I never had anything but cordial relations with him, I found myself wondering if he really liked the job, and I suspected that as a twice-divorced man with two grown children and a wine-distribution business on the side, he would land on his feet. (I also found it telling that he had been passed over for the department chair's job in favor of a younger colleague.) Rick was mad when Alan vetoed his proposal to increase the size of our department to allow us to have an anthropology elective — he would teach it, and someone would take over his survey sections — but since there was an effective hiring freeze across the school, I don't know why he had ever thought approval was likely. And math teacher Elsa Chang was a lovely woman who was deadly dull, so it was probably right that she was denied tenure, notwithstanding the outcry it engendered, one surely intensified by lingering bad feelings surrounding Danny's firing, even though Alan merely approved, rather than recommended, Elsa's termination (some suspected he pressured the chair to make the move). The depth of the distrust that seemed to envelop Alan struck me as a cheap form of populism whereby teachers cast themselves as speakers of truth to power. What I saw was complaining as a form of entitlement.

On the other hand, I couldn't quite bring myself to endorse Alan's leadership. Though he was always courteous in conversation and graceful in expression, there was something about the man that made it hard to embrace his style, an insularity of manner that carried with it a whiff of (racial?) distrust — unless, of course, I was projecting my own distrust back on him. But admitting that possibility didn't make it any easier to cast my lot with him.

And yet at the sullen, awkward faculty meeting billed as a "town hall" with Alan that had preceded our trip to the bar that Friday afternoon, I found myself sympathizing with Alan as he talked about things like fundraising and the upcoming accreditation process. When he made his plea that we give him the benefit of the doubt—presumably in regard to appointing committee members to head the evaluation effort, but surely heard as a veiled request to put the Danny Miller situation behind us—I came very close to standing up in front of my colleagues and expressing a sentiment I'd spent about fifteen minutes formulating: "Yes, Alan, I do think we should give you the benefit of the doubt, because an unwillingness to begin from a supposition of good intentions will lead us into a ditch of cynical paralysis." By that point I'd become sick of the sniping—and I'd become sick of my own indecision. But I could not get myself to rise from my chair and say something I feared would just sound as rehearsed as it was. I wasn't sure my opinion would carry much weight—and I wasn't sure my own reputation could afford an act of solidarity across the faculty-administration divide. So I played it safe, and two hours later found myself embarrassed by my colleague Denise's ability and willingness to brave her colleagues' disapproval, allowing Rick's barely veiled aggression to roll off her. I paid no obvious price for my flight to the men's room, and by the time I got back the conversation had shifted to the weekend's football games. But I wouldn't have been surprised if Rick had made some cutting remark about me while I was gone, and I strongly suspected that if I'd heard what it was, the knife, in the words of an old song I loved, would feel like justice.

❦

It had been a miserable field trip for the three sections of our humanities course. The weather had been terrible—raw, windy, raining—pretty much wiping out the walking tour portion of our plans. We huddled in doorways as students gave presentations about nearby sites too soggy to actually visit. Two kids had gotten into a fistfight; a third had stomach trouble and threw up on the edge of Central Park. Our buses were delayed in meeting us at the pickup point. Then about two miles from school, one began to have mechanical problems and the driver had to pull over to the edge of the highway. After the drivers conferred with each other by cell phone, it was agreed that our driver would bring us back to school and then return to retrieve the teachers and students on the other bus.

Our bus arrives in near-darkness. The religion colleague with whom I teach the course, Jerry Green—a good guy—has offered to linger, ensure that kids make their connections with their parents, and wait for the second bus so that my English colleague Denise Richardson and I can go home. I accept gratefully (I can feel a cold coming on), but before I can leave I need to check in with the bus driver and sign off on the necessary paperwork, which I do while everyone else gets off the bus. When I disembark into a misty rain, the parking lot is full of cars idling with headlights on, along with parents milling around the lot waiting to retrieve their children. There are also clusters of parents standing near Jerry to seek information about the stalled bus, though presumably most of their children had called to explain.

I'm about to head to my car when I see Jerry listening to an angry parent who holds an umbrella in one hand and points at him with a cell phone in the other. "Thirty-five goddamned minutes," he's saying. "Who the hell is in charge here?"

"Can I help you?" I ask, striving for my most neutral tone.

The man—short, wiry, dark eyes, jet-black hair with gray accents, olive overcoat over a suit—turns to look at me. "I don't know. *Can* you?"

"What seems to be the problem?"

"What seems to be the *problem*? Where is my daughter? Why are you so late? Why does no one seem to know what they're talking about? Is that enough of a *problem* for you?"

"I was explaining that the bus broke down," Jerry says.

"And what I want to know is: what's the plan?" He shook his cell phone. "Why has no one informed me about what has happened? Why has no one told me how you are going to address this situation? Why is there no accountability?"

"Couldn't you call your daughter?" Jerry asked.

"She's not answering her phone. But that's not the point. The point is that you people don't seem to know what the hell you're doing."

I could feel my restraint ebbing. "Look. It's been a long day. We're all a little tired. But we've got this situation under control—"

"When am I going to get my daughter back?"

"You see that bus? It's leaving right this instant to go retrieve your daughter. She's about ten minutes away. I figure she'll be back here in about twenty minutes, tops."

"So you're telling me that she's going to be an hour late."

"Jesus, mister. We didn't want the bus to break down. You have to wait an hour, you wait an hour. This isn't something we could have foreseen."

"What's your name?"

I am angry. I reach for my wallet. "Horace Dewey. Chair of the history department, aka the guy in charge here. Take my card. Please. Contact anybody you like." Asshole.

"Oh I will. I most certainly will."

"Wonderful," I say sarcastically. "Good fucking night!"

"Hey!" he says, angrily calling after me, but I don't look back from walking to my car. "This is not over," he's shouting. "I can assure you of that." I thrust my hand into my pocket, fishing for my keys. Better that than act on my impulse to stick up my middle finger. Finally, this godforsaken ordeal is over.

Except that it isn't. I wake up the next morning to find a string of e-mails waiting for me. The first, in reverse order, is from Alan Sanders. "Horace," he wrote, "We need to confer regarding a parent complaint. Make an appointment with Doris." The second, from my principal, Hannah Osborne, says, "I need to hear your side of the story in last night's dispute before I talk with Alan. Stop by sometime this morning." And the third is from the parent in question, a man by the name of Simon Levenson. *Oh shit,* I think as I scroll down in panic. *I am Danny Miller.*

"I have been a parent at this school for twelve years," Levenson begins in a missive addressed to Alan and Hannah. "And never once have I ever been subjected to such shocking treatment or witnessed such shocking dereliction of duty." Levenson describes a scene of chaos — late buses, anxious parents, an inability to get direct answers to simple questions. He is appalled that that I would simply leave the scene. (I do feel a twinge of guilt about that, though mostly that I shouldn't have let Jerry shoulder the burden by himself.) And he is deeply offended that I addressed him using "the f-word." Levenson describes me as "seeming to regard myself as beyond accountability" and calls on the administration to demonstrate that this is not the case.

"Did you tell him to go fuck himself?" Hannah asks after I go to her office before school and explain what happened. She seems both incredulous and amused.

"No, not directly. I said 'Good fucking night,' which was really more an expression of exasperation about how the day went than something directed at him." There is some truth to this.

She chuckles. "Well, he sounds like a prig to me." I admire the inner censor that makes Hannah say "prig" instead of "prick." She looks down at her computer, apparently at the e-mail. "But it turns out he's kind of a macher." Years of Manhattan living have led Hannah, a Unitarian Universalist from Maine, to embrace Yiddish slang. "Levenson is a big donor. Alan is going to have to massage his ego. But I think this is going to be OK."

Think this going to be OK? My heart sinks. And it doesn't rise any when I explain the situation to my wife. "How you could you be so stupid?" she asks. "You *know* Sanders has a low tolerance threshold for offensive language. I'm really angry at you, Horace. We literally can't afford for you to be so careless." She later apologizes for her lack of sympathy for me. But I understand her fear, because I share it.

The one bright spot is my colleagues. Jerry tells me that he's written a strongly supportive e-mail to Hannah and Alan, and the story of my encounter seems to have made me folk hero for a day.

"Good fucking morning!" Denise says to me brightly by the coffee machine.

"Hey, nice job with Simon Levenson," Troy tells me. "Lily Levenson is lovely, but the dad is impossible. I overheard him at a volleyball game last year pontificating about the evil of teachers' unions—this from a Citibank guy! She's now in Eddie's class, and he tells me he's still a jerk."

My most satisfying moment comes the following morning when I feel a hand on my back as I'm eating a bowl of oatmeal.

"Horace fucking Dewey," Rick says to me, drawing out each syllable, as a few other teachers in front of me look on approvingly. "Bravo, Horace. Didn't think you had it in you." I note the passive aggression, but I can't help but revel in Rick's approbation. I may not like the man, but I want him to like me.

My appointment with Alan comes later that afternoon. "Good to see you, Horace," he tells me as his secretary, Doris Chen, ushers me into his office. The sun streams in on an elegantly furnished room, one wall of which is painted a surprisingly dark blue. "Have a seat." I choose a Windsor chair; Alan, who is wearing an expensive silk vest, sits on a small couch. His desk, behind him, sports a photograph of a handsome (second) wife and two daughters, the oldest of whom I believe attends the middle school, one grade ahead of my daughter and one grade behind my son. I had forgotten about that. We make some of the obligatory small talk: weather lousy, classes going fine, et cetera.

After a decent interval I cut to the chase: "Alan, I'm really sorry about this whole situation. Regardless of any explanation I have, I really regret the fact that you and Hannah had to get involved in the first place."

"There's no need to apologize, Horace."

"No, really. It's important to me that any mistakes I make are ones that can be contained and resolved by myself."

"I understand that, Horace. And it says good things about you. As does Hannah's support for you. She told me what you had told her, which sounds very reasonable. I think we all agree you should not have said what you did. But we don't need to make a federal case out of it. You had a long day; he was understandably anxious about his child. But everything turned out fine."

"I'm not sure Mr. Levenson would agree."

"As it turns out, I ran into Simon yesterday. We had a board meeting. And you're right: Simon feels like we need to have more backup systems in place. But I'm satisfied that the situation was handled adequately, and I told him that we had to agree to disagree."

"Wow. I don't know what to say."

"You don't need to say anything. I told Simon that you were among the most dedicated teachers at the school. He said he had heard that. In fact, he said, his biggest problem is his daughter, who's convinced you're going to hate her because you had an argument with her dad. Simon asked if you would be willing to write her a short note and say that there will be no hard feelings if she ever takes one of your courses."

"Absolutely. I hear she's a sweet kid."

"Well, I imagine you'd write her even if she wasn't." There's mirth in his eyes.

"Yes, of course." There's none in mine. "I really appreciate your support here, Alan."

"Think nothing of it. It's easy to support you, Horace. Which is good, because I'd like to avoid firing anyone for a while." He breaks into a grin and stands up: my cue to go.

"He bought you cheap," my wife tells me over dinner that night. "Not that there's much you can do for him. But at least you're one member of the faculty who's not going to be bad-mouthing him."

"Well, I wasn't really bad-mouthing him before."

"No. And he probably knew that. But he probably also knows you haven't exactly been his vocal champion, either. Now you have a reason to be grateful to him, which will make it just a little easier to marginalize his critics. Some of those critics will see the way he handled you as manipulative. But others — like Denise — may be more willing to give him the benefit of the doubt now. In any case, he has your number, Horace. So, for that matter, does Rick. You're a nice guy, sweetheart. But you're a lame political infighter."

"Thanks?"

"You're welcome. Now get back to work."

I did.

BROWNIE POINTS

"You see Jasmin's eyes?" Mario Imperioli nudges me while we're standing at the back of the dining hall of the camp facility.

Jasmin Thompson is sitting at a crowded table about fifteen feet away. At the moment I focus my gaze on her, she's laughing hard with her eyes closed while putting her hands on the shoulder of Mark Jacero, our star tight end (headed to Colby on a football scholarship). I've never taught Jasmin; my dim sense of her is solely the product of a six-week, lecture-intensive SAT II prep course I offered on Saturday mornings a year and a half ago. She came bleary-eyed with a venti Starbucks, never said a word. "Can't say I see much there," I reply to Mario.

"I know that look." Mario, who teaches in the math department, says. He's about fifteen years younger than me with a three-month-old daughter. "The glassy eyes. Been there myself once or twice." He reaches into his pocket and pulls out his cell phone. "Be right back."

Mario starts taking what seems to be random pictures of different tables. But after a few shots he turns his focus to Jasmin's table. "*Hiiii* Mr. Imperioli," Sarah Jenkins says," waving languidly and laughing at what seems to be an inside joke. Mario doesn't acknowledge the greeting but snaps away. A couple kids at the table smile for him, but most don't pay any attention. He comes back to my side. "May come in handy," he says. "Look, the food line has gotten shorter. Let's grab some grub."

We're on a somewhat unusual overnight field trip. By long-standing custom, rising seniors go on a rafting trip in the Delaware Water Gap in the closing days of August. But a freakishly heavy thunderstorm led to flooding and extensive power outage at the facility in southern New Jersey where we were booked to stay, and the school was forced to cancel the trip. I was delighted; as the adviser to a dozen of these seniors, I was expected to go and was dreading bad food, an uncomfortable bunk bed in a cabin with colleagues, and supervisory responsibilities. Naturally, the presidents of the senior class led a crusade to reschedule the event, and the administration relented, organizing another trip to the campsite, sans rafting, on a Sunday-Monday in mid-May. I would have a partial dispensation; on the second day of the trip I was already booked to address a group of college admissions officers who would be visiting East Hudson as part of a panel discussing writing curricula. This meant I could drive my own car down to the camp rather than ride the bus, and maybe get reimbursed for a meal as well as the gas. More important, it meant I could leave first thing in the morning in order to get back in time for the session, which was scheduled for 10:00 a.m.

I can't say it's been a bad day. Actually, the weather in the days preceding the trip have been usually warm and humid, though I've been warned that it gets quite cool here in the woods at night. Everyone is apparently at lunch when I pull into the parking lot, but I run into a friend, visual arts teacher Troy Ricci, who's headed to the cabin we've been assigned to share. "They have a pool here and it's open," Troy tells me. "What do you say you and I get a swim in before the kids get back from lunch?"

"Tempting," I say sincerely. "But I didn't bring a bathing suit."

"You got shorts?"

"I do."

"Well, then, you're off to the races."

I'm inclined to hesitate, but the prospect of a swim, my favored form of summer exercise, is appealing, and Troy is making it more so. Without his prodding I probably wouldn't go ahead with it, but the knowledge that time is short—I don't particularly want to be parading around youthful bodies in my distinctly middle-aged one—means I can't hesitate. So I decide to take the plunge, changing into a pair of gym shorts and grabbing a towel, a T-shirt, and a copy of the *New Yorker*, which I leave at a picnic table just inside the fenced-in pool area. The pool itself, which is surprisingly large, is empty except for a single lifeguard (must be back early from college). It also has lap lanes. I get a dozen in before the first students start to arrive. I come up for air at the edge to find myself looking up at Isabel Ravitch wearing a mint green bikini. I remember walking behind the raven-haired Isabel, who plays volleyball, one day and reckoning that she's almost six feet tall. In my semisubmerged state, I'm a little awed by the sight of her.

"Nice *job*, Mr. Dewey! Love that breaststroke!"

"How are you, Isabel?"

"Great!"

"Izzy! Look, there's water guns!"

Mark Jacero, whose magnetism will soon prove irresistible to Jasmin Thompson, is calling her, and Isabel leaves me behind without a second thought. I hop out of the pool and make a beeline for my towel and T-shirt. By now a couple students have jumped into the pool (Troy is floating on his back), but it's still largely empty. I sit down at the picnic table; I figure maybe I can get in a quick skim through the "Talk of the Town" section of *the New Yorker* before I officially check in with Letty Aronson, the twelfth-grade dean, for whatever chaperoning tasks she may have to delegate.

I appear to have dozed off. When I awake, I see Letty sitting poolside, her khakis rolled up, legs in the water. She's wearing an East Hudson homecoming T-shirt and beach cap and looks like she's luxuriating in her own backyard—a little dumpy-looking, but utterly at ease with herself and the students, some of whom are arranged on either side of her conversing pleasantly and quietly. I envy Letty: she's so comfortable with herself and these kids. Which is why, of course, she's so good at her job. I shift my gaze slightly and see another group of students squealing and wrangling with each other over the water guns, their bodies in unselfconscious contact. Letty turns her head and sizes up the situation, apparently deciding she doesn't need to intervene. I know I should be getting up, but something seems to be holding me in place. I feel like there's a pane of glass separating me from this idyll. I'm in this world but not of it.

"Hey Mr. Dewey—I didn't know you were on this trip." It's my advisee Robbie Menzies. I explain the circumstances of my arrival, ask him how he's doing, throw him some questions about the Mets (he's a huge fan, and I've got enough basic literacy to ask about their pitching prospects and whether this year's free-agency acquisitions will make any difference). He's explaining how excited he is to be headed to Davidson in the fall—Division III school with Division I spirit—when I see Letty headed my way. "Horace," she says evenly. "I didn't realize you had arrived."

I hear this as oblique, and fair, criticism. "Sorry, Letty. Actually been here for a while."

She continues to look at me evenly, nodding slightly, in a way I find a little unnerving. But then she seems to put any pique behind her. "Well, that's good. We're in the middle of free time now. Check in with Ian and Mindy to make sure they don't need any help over by the lake or the ball fields. I'll need you at the dining hall no later than 4:45 to help with dinner."

Which is how I find myself with Mario, who's taking pictures. I see him walk over to the other side of the room to confer with Troy, who turns his head sharply and squints in reply to what Mario has said. Troy, in turn, goes and whispers to the other chaperones. He talks for a while with Ian Kot, another math teacher who coaches the Frisbee team. Do the students know we think there's something up? If so, they give no sign.

"Ian thinks it's Alexi Rothkopf," Mario says upon his return. "She apparently made a pan of pot brownies that were distributed at some point this afternoon."

I only know Alexi by sight. One of the Beautiful People: expensive clothes and makeup. "How many kids do you think ate them?"

"No idea. We're going to have to be on the lookout at the campfire tonight." He chuckles. "Maybe we should monitor s'mores consumption."

I've only had pot brownies once in my life. I was in college, hanging out with a bunch of friends in our apartment. I had just about concluded the brownies had no effect when suddenly I felt clobbered by the high while we were walking around campus. It was fun, but I never felt compelled to do it again. (My sole experience with cocaine was scarier because I could see just how compelling it would be to do it again—and again and again.) How is it for these kids? Do girls like Jasmin Thompson feel the impact sooner because they're smaller? I'm tempted to ask Mario but decide I don't want to reveal how clueless I am.

I remain clueless by the bonfire, which roars as the air chills and the light grows dark. There's the usual raucousness along with a series of heartfelt testimonials. "I just want to thank you guys for always being there for me," Tiffany Broadie says.

"Ms. Aronson, you have no idea how much a difference you've made in my life," Perry Adams says.

"SENIORS! This is our *time!*" Jacero says amid much cheering. "Let's make our mark. Let's do it so that someone will say, 'Remember Mark Jacero from the class of 2016?'" There's good-natured booing at this. Is he stoned or just the good-natured egomaniac I've always known him to be?

"What are you hearing?" I ask Mario after spotting him with my flashlight after the campfire breaks up and students head to their cabins.

He shrugs. "There's shit going on, but so far I can't point a finger at anyone. We'll have to see how the night goes." He and I make our assigned rounds without incident.

Sometime about 11:30, Troy and I make a small campfire outside our cabin, at which point Adam Edelstein and Jay Rothko, who are staying nearby, amble over, as does Mario. They're supposed to be under curfew, but we let them linger. They're eager to compare high school students of the 2010s with those of the 1990s, a subject in which Mario has more authority than I do. They seem painfully earnest — even more earnest than I was at their age (really, don't they have anything better to do than hang out with the likes of us?). When the smoke from the fire begins to blow in my face, I wander back inside and lie on the bottom bunk. I probably should still be out there, but I figure Troy will summon me if he or anyone else needs me.

When I wake up in the black, silent cabin, I pull out my cell phone: 4:17. *You know,* I tell myself, *I don't really have to stay. Everyone understands that I'm supposed to be gone in the morning, so why not leave now?* I turn on my flashlight and rustle around a bit, but Troy is dead to the world. How late was he up? As I make my way to the parking lot, I hear voices murmuring but no sign of any disturbance. I'm pleased to sail across the George Washington Bridge a little after 6:00, with time to go home and shower before the college symposium. I struggle to stay awake, a struggle I would no doubt have even if I wasn't working on only four hours of sleep. I get a little jolt when my phone vibrates just as I'm about to doze off. I take a surreptitious look. It's a text from Hannah Osborne. "Come by my office when you're done today," it says.

By the time I arrive at the principal's suite, at about 4:30, her door is closed. though I look in the window and see all the chaperones there. They must have come straight from the bus; they look tired and irritable. Hannah waves me in. Ian nods in silent greeting. "I've been getting an update," she explains. "Mario called me from the bus, and he sent me some of the pictures he took on his phone. I'm appalled by this, and I'm trying to figure out what we should do."

"I don't see what we *can* do," Mindy Kallstrom says. "Can you really indict someone on the basis of glassy eyes?"

"I agree," Troy says. "Our evidence is far too inconclusive."

"What I'm wondering," Letty says, seeming to ignore them, "is whether we can or should make a distinction between those who brought the brownies and those who ate them."

"Do you think we could get anyone to admit that Alexi was the one?" Mario asks. "And if anyone did, could we do anything about it?" He, like Letty, seems to be looking for angles of pursuit, though neither has a workable lead.

"Maybe we can bring her in for questioning," Troy says, with just a hint of ironic policeman bravado. "Or we can haul Jasmin in here and get her to plead to a lesser charge in exchange for her testimony."

Hannah is shaking her head. "No," she says. "That won't work." I'm surprised she seems to be taking Troy seriously.

"Did anything happen after we all turned in?" I ask. "Were there any incidents?"

"Nothing overt," Letty says. "At about 1:00 a.m. I went over to one of the girls' cabins because I heard someone throwing up. It was Sarah Jenkins. I went to the bathroom and asked if she needed help. But she said she was OK. 'I think I have a stomach bug,' she told me. 'My brother had it. But I'll be fine.' If she'd smoked a joint I could work with her breath. But under the circumstances I had nothing. And the rest of the girls were mum."

"Seriously," Mindy says, "I think they pulled off the perfect crime. If we start making accusations without good evidence, we're going to look worse than tyrannical. We'll look incompetent."

"We can't do nothing," Mario says. "*That* will make us look incompetent. And encourage the other kids to do this kind of thing again. I'm thinking that the one thing we have going for us is that they don't *know* what we've got on them."

There's a long silence. Hannah has turned her head and seems to be looking out the window toward the quad. "I think Mario is onto something," she says, still gazing into the quad, where a pair of students are playing catch with a Frisbee. Then she turns her attention back to us. "What about this?" she says. "We tell them that we have evidence of marijuana use on the field trip. We offer them a deal. If they come forward and admit it, they will forfeit their right to go to the prom. But that will be the extent of their punishment, and the incident will not be reported to their colleges. If, however, they don't come forward and we have or acquire proof of their involvement, everything is on the table."

"You mean expulsion, no diploma, notifying the colleges," Mario says. He and Hannah seem to be communicating telepathically. She nods.

"Wow," Mindy says. I can't tell if she's reacting to the severity of the scenario or Hannah's cleverness. I'm focused on the latter.

Troy asks, "How about they get to go to the prom if they're willing to provide evidence for us?"

"No." Hannah is firm. "We're not going to go McCarthyist on them. Kids hate snitches, and I don't blame them. This will be about them reckoning with their own choices and weighing consequences."

Letty is nodding her head. "I like it. How are you going to get the word out?"

"You are," Hannah says. "Send out an e-mail to the whole grade. Tell them that Ms. Osborne is supervising an investigation regarding illicit activity on this weekend's overnight trip. An air of mystery will help here."

Another silence. "We agree, then?" Hannah asks. There are murmurs of agreement. "So let's do it," she says. "Letty, tell them they have ten days to come forward, after which the offer is rescinded."

"Are you afraid no one will come forward?" I ask.

"It's possible," she says. "That's a risk. But as Mindy has pointed out, we don't have a lot of cards to play. That outcome is only marginally worse than pretending it never happened. At the very least there are going to be people who sweat out the next few weeks. I suspect we'll net a few." She looks around the room. "God, you people look like you need a shower and a drink." Hannah opens a drawer in her desk and pulls out her purse. She hands an Amex card to Letty. "Go ahead and forge my signature," she tells her. "Any of you who want to head over to Jake's can have a burger and a glass of wine on my discretionary fund."

I'd love to go. But my daughter's soccer practice and unfinished laundry beckon. My wife wouldn't be happy to have me gone for dinner two nights in a row. One more way I'm on the periphery of all the interesting stuff. I remind myself that the company of my family will outlast the company of my coworkers.

Letty's e-mail goes out the next day. The buzz on campus is palpable. Robbie Menzies asks me during advisory if I think Hannah is being fair. When I say yes, he agrees. The day after that, two students come forward to confess. Three days later, another two do. There's no action for a couple days after that, but as the deadline nears, clumps of students come clean. By the closing of the deadline a stunning 27 students out of a class of 151 won't be going to the prom. Among those who will: Alexi Rothkopf. With Mark Jacero.

Prom night finds me at the Puck Building, site of our annual rite of passage. Senior advisors (which is to say all those who went on the field trip a few weeks earlier) are on a receiving line, shaking hands and embracing the parade of tuxedos and gowns. "I wonder what the East Hudson Twenty-Seven are doing tonight," I muse to Mindy amid a pause in the action.

"You didn't hear?" she asks, incredulous. "Jasmin Thompson's dad rented a yacht in Martha's Vineyard for them. I saw some of the pictures he posted on Facebook when I was riding the bus down here."

SCHOOL'S CLOSE

REGRADUATING

I make a detour to look at the quad when I arrive at school for a final round of faculty meetings. Surprisingly, there are no obvious traces of yesterday's ceremonies. Less than twenty-four hours ago, this space was teeming with parents, grand-parents, alums, and hundreds of students, some of whom were wearing caps and gowns and about to dissolve into living ghosts. Today all that remains is a sole folding chair. And since it's brown, not black like the hundreds that had been set up, I'm not even sure it was here yesterday. The only sign that anything out of the ordinary has happened are the distressed stripes of grass running horizontally across the quad. The maintenance crew will take care of that in pretty short order, and this space will revert to a space of silence, punctuated only by the occasional round of elementary school day-campers singing here on summer afternoons, or administrators walking to and from their cars. (There will also be a new program this year for entering high school students and current students at academic risk, in which I will be teaching. I'm nervous and excited about trying to stretch a little.) Birds and bees will hold dominion for a season.

I'm relieved it's finally over. It's been three weeks since the seniors finished classes, a period punctuated by end-of-the-year parties, final exams, the prom, the senior dinner, and other rituals. Graduation is the most tedious. People typically experience their own over a string of a dozen or so years: elementary school and middle school, then high school and college, followed perhaps by a graduate degree, each a little more bittersweet and dogged by anxiety. And then that's it for a generation. But we teachers (especially high school teachers) go through the process every year. The students, the speeches, the recitation of the school song—they all tend to run together. If anything is likely to be memorable, it's the weather: hot or rainy, surprisingly cool or surprisingly beautiful. There's usually a moment of genuine gladness at some point in the morning, as we witness visible signs of maturity in some of our charges. And there's often a moment of genuine regret, too, when we face an esteemed colleague's retirement, the graduation of the final child in a cherished family, or a fond farewell from a clutch of friends who complemented each other so nicely. Any of these people may reappear at some point, perhaps in some transfigured way. But the uncertainty of such scenarios and the certainty of time's passage make such moments bittersweet at best.

It's always a relief when you get in the car and head home after such rituals, and I'm glad to seize a life, however quotidian, that's truly my own. For years now, it's been my habit to come home from graduation and mow the lawn. I think of Winslow Homer's 1865 painting *Veteran in a New Field*, which depicts a recently returned Civil War soldier threshing wheat. Figuratively speaking, my campaign is over, and I'm eager to get back to my farm.

This experience of closure is among the greatest satisfactions of teaching. Other walks of life are comparably cyclical. But I don't think any afford the kind of clean lines and closed books that a life in schools does. Many working people take extended summer vacations, but few of them are as expansive and sharply chiseled as that afforded by an academic schedule. As we are all veterans of schooling, this experience is a virtual birthright. But only teachers refuse to relinquish it.

The time will come—unexpectedly quickly—when my longings will turn away from completion and repose toward the rebirth that comes with the fall. In my case, the longings typically return long before it's time to actually reenter the classroom. But as I make my way from meeting to meeting, from a final faculty softball game to a final trip to the local watering hole before we all disperse, I pause to savor the cadence. The present is past. And history will be born anew.

AFTERWORD

A Note on Context

Though this book is essentially an extended essay—or, in my fondest formulation, a set of interlocking essays that can be profitably read separately or as a whole—it emerged from a specific educational discourse. I'm not a professional scholar of education, nor have I received formal training from a certified education program or school. But I'd like to explain where I'm coming from intellectually, if for no other reason than to acknowledge some debts.

For a number of decades now—actually, well over half a century—the national conversation about education has been conducted with a sense of perceived urgency. And in that conversation, the state of the teaching profession has been central. Reformers have developed a wide array of proposals to improve pedagogic practices, ranging from carrots in the form of merit pay to sticks in the form of penalizing teachers whose students perform poorly on standardized tests, as well hybrids like Value Added Modeling (VAM), which seek to measure a teacher's contribution to student performance over time. In recent years curriculum mapping has also become a widespread technique to foster a collective adoption of what are called, with a nod toward pluralism but an unmistakable thrust toward quality control, "best practices."

Teachers are hailed as neglected public servants; they're excoriated as lazy bureaucrats insulated from accountability by their powerful unions. But left or right, good or bad, teachers are seen as the key to schooling. There have been voices, especially recently, of people who are beginning to wonder about this—those who ask, for example, whether prevailing social conditions in a community or the climate established by a school principal may be more important than the work of an individual teacher in shaping a student's experience[1]—but even they understand they're responding to the conventional wisdom about the centrality of teaching, wherever they may happen to position themselves with regard to it.

The national discussion about teacher performance is commonplace in the realms of mass media and campaign oratory, as well as in the dialogue between parent and child, making teachers a frequent topic of dinner table conversation. But this general-audience colloquy is merely the tip of a discursive iceberg. For over a century now, academe has also supported a large national intellectual infrastructure in which generations of experts have conducted research, articulated policy agendas, and sustained schools of education at major universities. Much of this work has a strong clinical component of teacher education, as well as data-driven studies that seek to document the efficacy of a particular approach to teaching. These efforts have been well chronicled in the scholarship of people like Lawrence Cremin and Diane Ravitch, who have charted the ebb and flow of educational reform.[2]

Much of the conversation about high school teaching in particular takes two forms. The first falls into the domain of pragmatic, how-to literature in the spirit of Ralph Tyler's classic *Basic Principles of Curriculum and Instruction* over a half-century ago.[3] Such work is designed to introduce neophytes into the profession, providing pedagogical frameworks and brass-tacks advice as well as tips and tricks designed to appeal to rookie and veteran alike. Most of these fall into the textbook market. But there are a few (the works of writers such as Sara Lawrence-Lightfoot and Robert Fried come to mind) who manage to break out of that niche and gain a foothold in the trade market.[4]

Then there are the reformers. They have produced a larger body of work that appeals to people interested in policy and politics in which teaching is only one, but often an important, component of their critiques. Some, like E. D. Hirsch and Diane Ravitch, command national audiences. Others, like Howard Gardner and Alfie Kohn, are not household names but have built brands and followings of real substance by dint of consulting and a steady flow of writing.[5]

What all these authors have in common is that they assert what teaching *should be*. With some exceptions, they are policy advocates, not teachers. Some of them *were* teachers (this sometimes functions as a credential that they use to press a case), but rarely do teachers write *as* high school teachers. Dan C. Lortie's rhetorical question of forty years ago continues to resonate: "How many famous teachers (classroom teachers, not professors or administrators) can a reader think of?"[6] He goes on to note that "a teacher today can be considered outstanding by those who are familiar with his work without being thought of as making a single contribution to knowledge of teaching in general; the ablest people in the occupation are not expected to add to the shared knowledge of the group." High school teachers sometimes react with ambivalence when they read the work of nonteaching experts or hear their speeches at schools or conferences. On one hand, teachers are often eager for bulletins from the wider field. On the other, they wonder how much relevance the opinions of experts really have — and they sometimes bristle when presented with advice they regard as unrealistic or condescending.

This skepticism can be a matter of defensiveness on the part of teachers, who are, as Lortie documented at some length, conservative in their temperaments (if not their politics). But it can also reflect the bona fide mysteries of the craft, which defy programmatic formulas. Tyler once elegantly defined education as "a process of changing the behavior patterns in people."[7] It *is* possible to get at this in a standardized test to some degree, particularly one that purports to measure critical thinking. But such a benchmark, as meaningful as it is elusive, defies longings for quantification, if for no other reason than the indefinite time horizon that measurement would require.

This refusal to acknowledge our faith in formulas leaves the progressive reformer in a dimly realized state of ignorance. In his book *Inside the Black Box of Classroom Practice*, Larry Cuban notes that despite a century of education reform, surprisingly little is understood about exactly what happens when the rubber of carefully orchestrated innovation hits the road of actual classroom practice. His answer: not as much as the reformers hope. In part, he says, that's because the fundamental structural components of schooling—things like teacher-centered instruction in age-graded schools supported by local property taxes—are facts of decisive importance that will often shape, if they don't actually inhibit or prevent, changes in secondary factors like a new curriculum. Cuban describes this as the metaphorical equivalent of refurnishing an existing house but keeping the same plumbing or heating system. And once in place, that new curricular furniture is likely to be rearranged by a particular classroom teacher and her students, none of whom are likely to inhabit it in precisely the same way. He dubs this combination of restless tinkering with little measurable change "dynamic conservatism."[8]

But Cuban sees the real source of misunderstanding about teaching practice as not simply structural but more decisively perceptual, even neurological. He makes a taxonomic distinction between tasks that are "complicated" and those that are "complex." Examples of the former are performing brain surgery and putting astronauts in space—they're extremely intricate undertakings that require the precise execution of a series of steps. Tasks that are complex, by contrast—like the instruction of the young—involve a series of unstable human behavioral variables operating simultaneously. Cuban feels that reformers too often think they're working with complicated institutions when in fact they're working with complex ones. He cites the work of Philip Jackson, who in *Life in Classrooms* wrote that "the path of educational progress more closely resembles the flight of a butterfly than the flight of a bullet."[9] My own preferred metaphor is that of teaching as a form of (jazz) musicianship—the classroom is the studio, and the curriculum is the score, which the teacher conducts in real time with a group of student players who respond to each other in a series of constant, overlapping, and improvisatory choices.

One of the more remarkable aspects of modern educational discourse is how little attention is actually paid to this musical dimension of everyday classroom experience—what actually gets said by student and teacher in a given discussion; what silent exchanges take place between them; what unacknowledged attitudes and assumptions shape the collective expression of a classroom culture. It's striking in this regard that Cuban cites Jackson, whose *Life in Classrooms* remains singular—almost fifty years after it was first published in 1968. Jackson introduces the second edition of his book, which focuses on primary school teaching, by explaining that he embarked on his study because he felt no one was doing this kind of work back *then*, either.[10]

In the decades since, a few writers about education have actually used dialogue and described close firsthand observation. Dan Lortie got close to this in his ethnographically sociological study *Schoolteacher* — a book that, unlike most, emphasizes the great uncertainty surrounding the teaching enterprise and the acute concern teachers have about whether they're reaching their students.[11] Katherine Simon captures actual classroom dialogue in her 2003 book *Moral Questions in the Classroom.*[12] But no writer was more successful in this regard than the late Ted Sizer, who repeatedly offered readers granular descriptions of exchanges between teachers, students, and administrators going about the work of schooling.[13] On the whole, however, such writing has been remarkably scarce, despite its distinguished pedigree. This book is an attempt to reassert its relevance, utility, and resonance.

Again, though: for all the power of their work, writers like Sizer were not actually teachers at the time they were producing such scholarship. Actually, there are some very good reasons for that. For one thing, the demands of a high school teaching job typically afford little time for the reading, research, and reflection necessary to produce a book, and little of the expectation to produce one that is incumbent, for example, on college professors (many of whom write books on teaching).[14] For another, any given classroom session is ephemeral, likely to be experienced as a good deal less than fascinating by the principal players in the room, not to mention an outsider entering midstream. More important, there are moral imperatives to protect the privacy of children, particularly when information may not be flattering. Even when candor might be legally possible, sheer self-preservation requires discretion in talking about bosses and colleagues. In his 2013 *Confessions of a Bad Teacher*, John Owens offers blunt assessments of his superiors, something only possible because he quit his job a few months into it.[15] It's not surprising that the most vivid and entertaining of teaching memoirs,

Frank McCourt's *Teacher Man*, describes encounters that took place decades earlier and was published after his retirement.[16] Sizer's famous protagonist, English teacher (and later principal) Horace Smith, is a fictional creation, though his experiences are based on real ones.

In a sense, this project attempts to function as a hybrid of Sizer and McCourt, fusing elements of memoir, anecdote, and analysis. By way of summary, I seek to accomplish three tasks:

1 Describe the work of teaching in ways that teachers will recognize, distilling and clarifying that work in a manner that will help them make any affirmations or adjustments they'd care to make;

2 Describe the work of teaching in ways that people considering the profession will find useful in terms of understanding its less discussed aspects and helping them decide whether to join it;

3 Describe the work of teaching so that those interested in offering a reform program will more fully recognize the realities they're seeking to bend toward improvement and take them into account as they formulate their different (and very possibly conflicting) approaches.

Note that the verb I use for each of these objectives is *describe*. Not *argue*, *demonstrate*, or *prove*. Maybe *explain*, but even when I do, it's going to be partial at best, because some things, metrics be damned, defy systematic explanation.

In the end, of course, the business — or, if you'll allow, the art — of teaching is not about teachers. It's about students. The final justification for trying to understand your own life's work is to help them understand theirs. And, in the process, to help them locate, and strengthen, the better angels of their nature.

ACKNOWLEDGMENTS

I am not at liberty to thank most of the people who made this book possible, for reasons explained in the author's note. Here I will simply state my deep and undying affection for the multiconstituency community I have designated the East Hudson School. The intelligence, grace, and goodheartedness of the people I have tried to bring to life on these pages can only be a pale reflection of the vitality I have experienced every day in my long but finite tenure there. "East Hudson": you have my eternal gratitude.

Though I worked in the publishing industry only briefly after graduating from college, I consider myself a lifelong student of that business. One of the things I've learned is that the great joy of a good editor involves accumulating and spending precious professional capital on long shots that just might — *might* — pay literal or figurative dividends. That Elizabeth Branch Dyson of the University of Chicago Press would see such possibilities in my over-the-transom query, e-mailed in an impulsive moment from a hotel lobby while visiting Milton Academy in December 2013, still strikes me as miraculous. While I don't have much hope that her confidence in me will pay off in any significant way, I do think the law of percentages will favor her over the long haul. I'll also take a moment here to express thanks for the insightful contributions of promotions manager Ryo Yamaguchi, director of promotions Levi Stahl, book designer Rich Hendel, and cover designer Isaac Tobin. Senior manuscript editor Ruth Goring made valuable editorial suggestions that went well beyond buffing my prose.

Readers will note that my unnamed family members are shadowy presences in this book, referred to individually as well as collectively. Rest assured that they have been a vital resource just offstage, fortifying me as well as making my respites worthwhile. They've all long accommodated themselves to my obsessive habits. I offer my thanks for their indulgence and my love.

"Horace Dewey"
Somewhere along the east bank of the Hudson
June 2015

NOTES

INTRODUCTION

1. Malcolm Gladwell, "Most Likely to Succeed: How Do We Hire When We Don't Know Who's Best for the Job?," *New Yorker*, December 15, 2008: http://www.newyorker.com/reporting/2008/12/15/most-likely-to-succeed-2, accessed May 21, 2015.

2. I realize in saying this I am staking out a (mild) position in a current intellectual debate. In her recent book *How Teaching Works (and How to Teach It to Everyone)* (New York: W. W. Norton, 2014), Elizabeth Green seeks to dismantle what she calls "the myth of the natural-born teacher" (p. 13), which she feels—plausibly enough—creates an counterproductive mystique around the profession and forestalls efforts to systematically improve professional development on a relatively large scale. Certainly, like any craft, teaching can be broken down into constituent parts that can be studied, practiced and perfected. But I would maintain, perhaps more readily than she would assent in an argument which is certainly nuanced, that there remains an element of irreducible talent involved in teaching akin to an aptitude for math, music, or management.

3. Tuition for the 2015–16 school year was $45,100. Assume an inflation rate of 4.5% annually (some years have been more, others less, always considerably more than the national rate of inflation) and the cumulative total is $892,260. By decade's end, it's likely that the total cost of an East Hudson education will top one million dollars.

4. Philip W. Jackson, *Life in Classrooms* (1968; New York: Teachers College Press, 1990), xxi.

5. For more on the way the teacher, even more than the curriculum, is, in effect, the message, see the study Jackson coauthored with Robert E. Boostrom and David T. Hansen: *The Moral Life of Schools* (1993; San Francisco: Jossey-Bass, 1998).

6. Jackson, *Life in Classrooms*, xx. The introduction of the second edition to *Life in Classrooms* was published in 1989.

COMPENSATIONS

1. On the role of women in the early teaching profession — and for a good overview of the teaching profession generally — see Dana Goldstein, *The Teacher Wars: A History of America's Most Embattled Profession* (New York: Doubleday, 2014). See especially chapter 1.

2. Statistical summaries, NYC Dept. of Education: http://schools. nyc.gov/AboutUs/schools/data/stats/default.htm, accessed November 30, 2014.

3. On the state of education and the relatively high status of teachers in other countries, see Amanda Ripley, *The Smartest Kids in the World — and How They Got That Way* (New York: Simon and Schuster, 2013).

SUBJECT MATTERS

1. *The Notebooks of F. Scott Fitzgerald*, edited by Matthew Bruccoli (New York: Harcourt Brace Jovanovich, 1978), 332.

NAME GAMES

1. J. D. Salinger, *The Catcher in the Rye* (1951; Boston: Little, Brown, 1991), 25.

GRADIENTS

1. The foremost scholars of authentic assessment are Jay McTighe and Grant Wiggins. See *Understanding by Design*, 2nd ed. (Upper Saddle River, NJ: Pearson, 2005).

PARENTAL TEACHING

1. Sara Lawrence-Lightfoot, *The Essential Conversation: What Parents and Teachers Can Learn from Each Other* (New York: Ballantine, 2004), 44.

HOME WORK

1. See, for example, Kohn's *The Homework Myth: Why Kids Get Too Much of a Bad Thing* (New York: Da Capo, 2008).

2. Amanda Ripley, *The Smartest Kids in the World and How They Got That Way* (New York: Simon and Schuster, 2013), 176–78.

3. For more on this, see Jim Cullen, *Essaying the Past: How to Read, Write and Think about History*, 2nd ed. (Malden, MA: Wiley-Blackwell,

2013), 76. Cullen got this definition of a thesis from Harvard University writing instructor Gordon Harvey.

4. See the National History Day website at www.nhd.org.

AFTERWORD

1. Diane Ravitch notes the limits of what teachers can do in *The Death and Life of the Great American School System: How Testing and Choice Are Undermining Education* (New York: Basic Books, 2010), 257–59; in "What Happens When Great Teachers Get $20,000 to Work in Low-Income Schools?" *Slate* reporter Dana Goldstein cites a McKinsey & Co. study that notes the appeal of a strong principal as a recruiting tool (slate.com, November 25, 2013).

2. Cremin is the author of a three-volume history of public schooling: *American Education: The Colonial Experience, 1607–1783* (New York: Harper and Row, 1972); *American Education: The National Experience, 1783–1876* (New York: HarperCollins, 1980), and *American Schooling: The Metropolitan Experience, 1876–1980* (New York: HarperCollins, 1990). He is also the author of *The Transformation of the School: Progressivism in American Education 1876–1957* (New York: Vintage, 1964). Among Ravitch's many books are *The Troubled Crusade: American Education, 1945–1980* (New York: Basic Books, 1985); *The Great School Wars: A History of New York City Public Schools* (1974; Baltimore: Johns Hopkins University Press, 2000); and *Left Back: A Century of Failed School Reforms* (New York: Simon and Schuster, 2000).

3. Ralph W. Tyler, *Basic Principles of Curriculum and Instruction* (1949; repr. Chicago: University of Chicago Press, 2013).

4. See, for example, Robert Fried, *The Passionate Teacher: A Practical Guide*, 2nd ed. (1995; Boston: Beacon, 2001), and Sara Lawrence-Lightfoot, The *Essential Conversation: What Parents and Teachers Can Learn from Each Other* (New York: Ballantine, 2004).

5. Hirsch is best known for his widely discussed *Cultural Literacy: What Every American Needs to Know* (Boston: Houghton Mifflin, 1987), which has spawned a series of more specific spinoffs. Gardner has become a cottage industry on the strength of *Frames of Mind: The Theory of the Multiple Intelligences*, 3rd ed. (1983; New York: Basic Books, 2011), which has spawned multiple sequels and related titles. Alfie Kohn is a progressive reformer best known for his criticism of homework. He became nationally prominent on the basis of *No Contest: The Case against*

Competition (orig. 1986; Boston: Houghton Mifflin, 1992) and many subsequent books.

6. Dan C. Lortie, *Schoolteacher: A Sociological Study*, 2nd ed. (orig. 1975; Chicago: University of Chicago Press, 2002), 241.

7. Tyler, *Basic Principles*, 5.

8. Larry Cuban, *Inside the Black Box of Classroom Practice: Change without Reform in American Education* (Cambridge, MA: Harvard Education Press, 2013), 2–3. The metaphor of a structural house and curricular furniture appears on p. 49.

9. Cuban, *Inside the Black Box*, 155; Jackson, *Life in Classrooms*, 166–67.

10. Jackson, *Life in Classrooms*, ix–xx.

11. See in particular chap. 6, "Endemic Uncertainties" (134–61), in Dan C. Lortie, *Schoolteacher: A Sociological Study*, 2nd ed. (orig. 1975; Chicago: University of Chicago Press, 2002).

12. Katherine G. Simon, *Moral Questions in the Classroom: How to Get Kids to Think Deeply about Real Life and Schoolwork* (New Haven, CT: Yale University Press, 2003).

13. Theodore Sizer, *Horace's Compromise: The Dilemma of the American High School* (Boston: Houghton Mifflin, 1984); *Horace's School: Redesigning the American High School* (Boston: Houghton Mifflin, 1992); *Horace's Hope: What Works for the American High School* (Boston: Houghton Mifflin, 1996). See also the book Sizer wrote with his wife Nancy Faust Sizer: *The Students Are Watching: Schools and the Moral Contract* (Boston: Beacon, 1999).

14. Among the best is Mark Edmundson. See *Teacher: The One Who Made the Difference* (New York: Random House, 2002). That book is about a high school teacher. Edmundson's 2013 book *Why Teach? In Defense of a Real Education* (New York: Bloomsbury) focuses on college teaching, though his analysis resonates widely. See also Jay Parini, *The Art of Teaching* (New York: Oxford University Press, 2005).

15. John Owens, *Confessions of a Bad Teacher: The Shocking Truth from the Front Lines of American Education* (Naperville, IL: Sourcebooks, 2013).

16. Frank McCourt, *Teacher Man: A Memoir* (New York: Scribner, 2005). The book was the third part of a trilogy that included McCourt's hugely successful *Angela's Ashes* (Scribner, 1996) and *'Tis* (Scribner, 1999).